LANGUAG
THE MIND

'This book is a very useful text that introduces key concepts and findings in psycholinguistics. The text covers the core areas from biological aspects of language to language acquisition and language processing, and should encourage students to delve more deeply into all of these areas. I recommend it very highly.'
Professor Martin Pickering, University of Edinburgh

Routledge Language Workbooks provide absolute beginners with practical introductions to core areas of language study. Books in the series offer comprehensive coverage of the area as well as a basis for further investigation. Each Language Workbook guides the reader through the subject using 'hands-on' language analysis, equipping them with the basic analytical skills needed to handle a wide range of data. Written in a clear and simple style, with all technical concepts fully explained, Language Workbooks can be used for independent study or as part of a taught class.

Language and the Mind

- is an accessible introduction to the relationship between language and mental processes
- covers core areas including language in the brain, language impairment, how language is acquired, how the mind stores vocabulary and how it deals with speaking, listening, reading and writing
- draws on a variety of real-life material
- employs a discovery approach that enables students to form conclusions for themselves
- can be used to complement existing textbook material

John Field teaches, writes and researches on the psychology of language and on Second Language Acquisition. His previous publications include *Psycholinguistics* (Routledge, 2003) and *Psycholinguistics: the key concepts* (Routledge, 2004). He currently teaches at Birkbeck College, London and the University of Reading and is a Teaching Fellow at the University of Leeds. He is convenor of the psycholinguistics group within the British Association of Applied Linguistics.

LANGUAGE WORKBOOKS

Series editor: Richard Hudson

Books in the series:

LANGUAGE AND THE MIND

JOHN FIELD

Routledge
Taylor & Francis Group

LONDON AND NEW YORK

First published 2005
by Routledge
2 Park Square, Milton Park, Abingdon, Oxon OX14 4RN

Simultaneously published in the USA and Canada
by Routledge
270 Madison Ave, New York, NY 10016

Routledge is an imprint of the Taylor & Francis Group

Typeset in Galliard and Futura by
Florence Production Ltd, Stoodleigh, Devon
Printed and bound in Great Britain by
TJ International Ltd, Padstow, Cornwall

British Library Cataloguing in Publication Data
A catalogue record for this book is available from
the British Library

Library of Congress Cataloging in Publication Data
Field, John, 1945–
    Language and the Mind/John Field.
       p. cm. – (Language workbooks)
    Includes bibliographical references and index.
    1. Psycholinguistics.   I. Title.   II. Series.
    P37.F488 2005
    401′.9–dc22   2004019525

ISBN 0–415–34185–X (hbk)
ISBN 0–415–34186–8 (pbk)

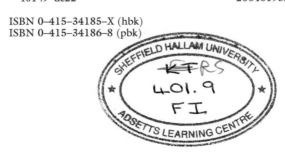

CONTENTS

USING THIS BOOK

You step into the road without seeing an oncoming car. A passer-by shouts '*Watch out!*', and you take a hasty step backwards. Underlying this apparently simple event is a complex operation that we tend to take for granted. All the speaker has done is to produce a string of sounds. It is *your mind* that distinguishes them from the noise of the traffic. They are in an entirely different category, one which human beings label speech. It is your mind that matches the sounds with those of the English language, breaks the string into words, retrieves meanings for those words and relates the whole to immediate circumstances.

An understanding of how the mind produces and receives language is critical to any study of what language is and how it operates. This workbook offers a basic introduction to this exciting and relatively new area of enquiry. PSYCHOLINGUISTICS, as it is known, can be a little daunting in the early stages because it combines two disciplines: language studies and psychology. Linguists sometimes find the psychological terms a nuisance and psychologists feel the same about the linguistic ones. This book aims to overcome such obstacles. It is designed specifically for those who are approaching the subject for the first time.

Psycholinguistics

It teaches through *discovery*: instead of providing long abstract explanations, it allows you to work out the essential ideas for yourself. The exercises invite you to explore your own language processes and to analyse examples of authentic spoken and written English. They give you insights into mental operations that you perform every waking hour, and they expand your understanding of how language functions.

The book assumes no prior knowledge of psychology and only a minimal knowledge of terms and ideas from language studies. You acquire the necessary information as you go. As well as exploring ideas from the psychology of language, the exercises develop some of the essential concepts that underlie the study of grammar, vocabulary or pronunciation. For example, when the way in which words are associated in the mind is examined in Unit 6, the terms that linguists use to describe these relationships are explained at the same time. Here, and elsewhere, the study of language use and language form go hand in hand.

If you feel at all unsure about a term that you come across, there are two reference sections at the end of the book to help. The first is a glossary that explains any basic linguistic terms in the book that you might have trouble with; the second is an index that indicates the unit in which a particular psycholinguistic term is first introduced and explained. To help you further, useful terms are highlighted in the text.

What exactly does the study of language and mind cover? At least five major areas can be identified, of which the first four are represented in this workbook.

(a)   whether language is peculiar to human beings, how language evolved, how the human brain handles language and what can go wrong with it;
(b)   how infants acquire language;
(c)   how words are stored in our minds and how we find them when we need them;
(d)   how we assemble words in order to express our thoughts and feelings and how we interpret the words of others;
(e)   how we succeed in learning foreign languages.

The first area (language and the brain) features in Unit 1, which considers whether or not animal communication is like human language. It is also covered in Unit 2, which looks at how the human brain handles language, and in Unit 5, which is about language disability.

Language acquisition

The second area is known as LANGUAGE ACQUISITION. Units 3 and 4 explore current ideas of how a child manages to acquire its first language so smoothly and rapidly. The approach presented in Unit 3 views language as a faculty that we inherit from our parents; while Unit 4 focuses instead on the interaction between carer and child.

We then go on to study two aspects of the mental dictionary, which provides us with building blocks for language in the form of words. The question in Unit 6 is: what information must we store about each individual word in order to use it accurately and appropriately? In Unit 7, it is: how do we find a word when we need it?

Language processing

Productive

Receptive

The later units of the book concern themselves with how we construct and understand pieces of language, a topic known as LANGUAGE PROCESSING. Each of the four language skills is explored in turn. Units 8 and 9 focus on the PRODUCTIVE skills of writing and speaking. Unit 10 looks at some of the basic principles that have guided thinking about language processing; and Units 11 and 12 apply these ideas to the study of the RECEPTIVE skills of reading and listening.

The point of the exercises in each of these units is to encourage you to think about the issues that arise and to develop your own views. For this reason, the answers to the exercises appear separately at the back of the book. Try not to turn to them until you have fully thought through the problem that is posed: the process of trying to find a solution is as important as the answer itself, if not more important.

The study of language and the mind relies very heavily upon examining and interpreting evidence – so, appropriately, each of the units has a proposal for a project that you might wish to carry out yourself.

Finally, there are suggestions at the end of the book for further reading, in case any of the topics particularly takes your interest and you want to follow it up. A short workbook like this can do little more than give a taste of what psycholinguistics offers – but you will certainly find ideas that fascinate, tantalise and, perhaps, encourage you to explore further.

John Field, London, 2004

ACKNOWLEDGEMENTS

I would like to thank all those who have so gamely tried out the activities in this book in talks that I have given in the UK and abroad. I think particularly of my present undergraduate class at Birkbeck College London, as well as earlier students who brightened some otherwise dismal conditions at Kings College London. I also recall a number of lively seminars with British and overseas teachers at International House and elsewhere.

For their support throughout the writing of the book, I owe a great debt to the Language and Linguistics team at Routledge. I especially mention Louisa Semlyen, who kept tabs on the project throughout despite the demands made by the arrival of Phoebe into this world, and Kate Parker, who responded with such enthusiasm to a tentative proposal on my part. I am also extremely grateful to Dick Hudson, the series editor, for his perceptive comments on an early draft and for so generously giving his time whenever we have had the opportunity to exchange ideas.

My personal thanks to Dr Jane Setter, a colleague at the University of Reading and a fine phonologist, for the spectrograms that appear as Figure 12.1. For permission to reproduce copyright material, the author and publishers would like to thank Terrance Deacon for Figure 2.3 and the MIT Press for Figure 10.1.

KEY TO IPA SYMBOLS

Consonants

Voiceless

p	pin
t	ton
k	cap
f	fan
θ	thing
s	sue
ʃ	ship
tʃ	chip

Voiced

b	bin
d	done
g	gap
v	van
ð	this
z	zoo
ʒ	measure
h	hit
dʒ	gym
m	met
n	net
ŋ	sing
w	wet
r	red
j	yet
l	let

Vowels

Short

ɪ	hit
e	head
æ	hat
ʌ	hut
ɒ	hot
ʊ	foot
ə	a(bout)

Long

iː	heat
ɑː	heart
ɔː	hoard
uː	hoot
ɜː	hurt

Diphthongs

eɪ	wait	əʊ	boat	ɪə	here
aɪ	tight	aʊ	bout	eə	there
ɔɪ	toy			ʊə	cure

Triphthongs

aɪə	fire	aʊə	flower

The variety of English illustrated is British RP.

LANGUAGE AND ANIMALS

1

An interesting branch of psycholinguistics investigates the question: is speech special? To put it another way: is language peculiar to human beings or do other species have forms of communication that resemble it?

This raises two more specific questions:

- Does natural animal communication resemble language?
- Can animals be taught to understand and to produce language?

EXERCISE

1.1   The brief introduction above made use of three terms that we must define at the outset. What do you understand by: SPEECH – LANGUAGE – COMMUNICATION?

SYSTEMS OF SIGNS

One way of examining communication is by considering it as a system of signs. Technically, the word SIGN refers to something that is used in order to represent something else. There are three types of sign relationship.

Sign

- An ICONIC sign resembles or depicts the object or action that it refers to. Example: the picture of a sun on a weather forecast chart.

Iconic

- An INDEXICAL sign is something that is closely associated with the object or action that it refers to. Example: smoke is an indexical representation of fire.

Indexical

Symbolic • A SYMBOLIC sign is something that stands for something else but otherwise bears no relationship to the object or action that it stands for. Example: a red traffic light means STOP.

Arbitrary Language is symbolic, unlike many other forms of communication. It is symbolic because the signs it uses – we call them words – are ARBITRARY. There is nothing inevitable that links the word ROSE to a particular kind of flower. If we all agreed to call the flower a SPLIDGE instead, it would not make any difference to the thing we were talking about.

EXERCISE

1.2 Here are a number of different forms of animal communication. In each case, decide whether the sign is iconic, indexical or symbolic.

(a) A dog scratches at the door.
(b) A bird sings to establish its territory.
(c) A snake hisses.
(d) A baboon shows its teeth.
(e) An eel signals its position and species by emitting an electrical impulse at a particular frequency.
(f) A cicada has a congregation call which invites other cicadas to join in with it in a chorus.

VOLUNTARY VOCALISATION

So, one way of distinguishing many types of animal communication from language is that they are not symbolic in the way that language is. A second distinction is illustrated by the anecdote below:

> Chimpanzees often produce food calls when they come upon a new food source. This stereotypic call attracts hungry neighbours to the location, often kin who are foraging nearby. [Jane] Goodall recounts one occasion where she observed a chimp trying to suppress an excited food call by covering his mouth with his hand. The chimp had found a cache of bananas ... and ... apparently did not want to have any competition for such a desirable food. Though muffling the call as best he could with his hand, he could not, apparently, directly inhibit the calling behaviour himself.
>
> (Deacon, 1997: 224)

EXERCISE

1.3 In what way can we say that this particular call is different from language?

Much animal communication is REFLEXIVE: it is like human coughing, laughter or tears, over which we can exercise little control.

Reflexive

There appears to be a marked difference in the brain configurations of animals and of human beings. The CORTEX or upper part of the human brain gives us a high degree of control over operations involving VOCALISATION. The same is not true in most mammals. Their cortices include areas that control movements of the mouth, tongue and lips, but the movements concerned are for the purposes of eating and grooming rather than uttering calls. So many of their calls appear to be made without any deliberate intention on the part of the animal. When monkeys suffer brain damage, it may leave them unable to eat, but their calls are often unaffected.

Cortex

Vocalisation

DESIGN FEATURES

In 1963, the linguist Charles Hockett drew up a list of DESIGN FEATURES that characterise language, thus enabling us to make comparisons with other forms of communication. His list has been expanded by later commentators, reflecting current ideas of what language is and how it operates.

Design features

EXERCISE

1.4 Below are some of the more important features that characterise language. Two of them relate to issues raised in Exercises 1.2 and 1.3.

    The terms used are those introduced by Hockett and others. They are followed by a set of definitions. Can you work out which definition matches which term?

1	Displacement	5	Interchangeability
2	Arbitrariness	6	Duality of patterning
3	Semanticity	7	Control
4	Cultural transmission	8	Creativity

(a) We can construct completely new utterances that we have never heard before.

(b) Language is used intentionally – unlike involuntary noises such as coughing or laughing.

(c) Smaller units (e.g. sounds) are combined into larger ones (words).

(d) We can talk about things that are not present and visible.

(e) Languages are handed on from one generation to the next.

(f) A word need not resemble in any way the object or action that it refers to.

(g) The same individual can both send out and receive a message.

(h) Different symbols are used to refer to different concepts.

ANIMAL COMMUNICATION

Some forms of animal communication are said to resemble language in certain ways. Here are examples.

- Vervet monkeys have a repertoire of 36 vocal sounds. Among them is a set of three alarm calls which are used to warn of predators. One is used when the threat comes from a snake, one when it comes from a leopard or other large mammal and one when it comes from a bird of prey. The calls are evidently understood by other vervet monkeys, since they look in the direction (ground, trees or sky) from which the danger comes. The other vervets take up the call, passing on the alarm to those that are further away.

- Worker bees use a set of strange dances to pass on information about a source of nectar that they have discovered. If the source is within about 5 metres of the hive, they turn round in circles. If it is a short way away, they dance in a figure of 8. If it is further, they waggle their abdomens. In the second and third of these performances, the angle of the bee's body indicates the direction of the nectar relative to the position of the sun, though 'up' and 'down' cannot be demonstrated. The dance is only performed by worker bees and appears to be inherited genetically rather than learnt.

- Dolphins use a system of clicks to communicate under water. These irregular bursts of sound last for about a thousandth of a second and are not audible by human beings. But they act as a kind of radar and enable dolphins to locate objects (including food sources) very accurately. It is not clear to what extent the clicks represent a one-way transmission of information and to what extent dolphins are able to communicate with each other.

EXERCISE

1.5 Consider these three examples of animal communication in the light of the design features that you have just studied. In what ways do they resemble language? In what ways are they different?

TEACHING ANIMALS LANGUAGE

A different approach to this issue asks whether animals are capable of acquiring a human language. We need first to consider exactly what is meant by 'acquiring'.

EXERCISE

1.6 Consider the example of a dog which comes to recognise the word WALK. The word has always been associated with going out, so the dog becomes excited when it hears WALK and fetches its lead. To what extent can we say the dog has 'acquired' the word?

Now consider what might happen if the dog heard the word on several occasions when no walk took place. What might happen?

The reason the dog responded in the way it did was because it had formed an automatic association between a word and an event. This kind of process was much studied by a movement in psychology known as BEHAVIOURISM, which was influential in the first half of the twentieth century. BEHAVIOURISTS claimed that behaviour was highly automatic – the result of a process known as CONDITIONING in which a particular STIMULUS (in our example, the word WALK) becomes associated with a particular RESPONSE (the dog goes to get its lead). The classic example was Pavlov's dog, which learnt to associate the ringing of a bell with the arrival of food and began to salivate whenever it heard the bell.

Behaviourism
Behaviourists
Conditioning
Stimulus
Response

EXERCISE

1.7 The weakness of the behaviourist argument is well illustrated by another example of 'animal language'. Suppose a parrot is trained by a series of rewards in the form of nuts to say *Good morning* whenever the cover is taken off its cage at the beginning of the day. To what extent has it learnt the concept behind the phrase?

In assessing whether an animal has or has not acquired a human language, we need to take account of at least three questions.

- Can the animal produce language as well as understand it?
- Can the animal use words as part of a system? The system might, for example, specify that words must occur in a certain order. Can it use the system creatively, to make new combinations?
- Does the animal recognise the symbolic nature of language? The word TABLE does not usually refer to a single table but to a whole class of objects that share certain features.

EXERCISE

1.8 Read the description below of how researchers managed to train a bonobo (pigmy chimpanzee) called Kanzi to communicate. Consider the results in terms of the three criteria just mentioned.

Does the study show that some primates can, in fact, acquire human language? Give arguments for and against. You may wish to think about what it is that motivates an animal like Kanzi to use language. Compare what a child has achieved in terms of language when it is the same age as Kanzi. Take account of the fact that the information that Kanzi was taught is a product of the human mind.

A CHIMP STUDY

Researchers have had varying degrees of success in training chimpanzees and other primates to communicate in ways that resemble language. One problem is that primates are physiologically incapable of vocalising the sounds of human speech. Instead, training projects today often get them to use a huge keyboard linked to a computer. The keyboard consists of a large number of keys of different colours bearing abstract shapes; and each is used to refer to an object or action in the real world. The keys are not marked in any way that associates them with the word that they refer to (i.e. there is no picture of a banana on the BANANA key).

In the mid-1990s, one research team announced a breakthrough with a bonobo called Kanzi. Kanzi had been present from a very young age during the rather unsuccessful training of his foster mother. When it came to his turn to be trained, he showed that he already knew many of the keyboard associations. This appeared to give him a head start. In all, he mastered about 400 symbols without the extended trials that had been necessary with other chimps. He could even group them into sets (e.g. FOOD and DRINK).

Kanzi's performance was monitored closely for 5 months when he was about five and a half years old. He produced more than 13,000 utterances during this period, of which around a tenth consisted of two words. Here, he showed signs of having acquired a set word order, in which an action preceded an object (GIVE BANANA) and even of applying that order to new situations and new combinations of words.

Remarkably, around 5 per cent of Kanzi's utterances at this time were spontaneous rather than responses to an exchange started by a trainer. Furthermore, he proved to be capable of responding correctly to around three-quarters of spoken sentences uttered by his trainers.

PROJECT

Study the system of communication used by one species. Possible subjects are primates, bees, birds, dolphins or whales. Suggested approaches:

(a) Obtain wildlife video footage showing the animals communicating.

(b) Contact your local zoo, wildlife area or safari park. Interview keepers about their experience of how the species communicates, and their views of how effective this communication is.

(c) Assess to what extent the system of communication resembles language.

2 LANGUAGE AND THE BRAIN

If, as seems likely, human beings are the only species that has a language, we might find an explanation in the different circumstances in which humans live, and their greater need for some form of social communication. An alternative view holds that humans have been able to evolve language because their brain is different from those of other species. We could also, of course, turn that last idea on its head and speculate that the human brain differs from those of other species *as a result of* employing language.

A different reason for studying the relationship between language and the brain comes from those with an interest in language acquisition. It is very difficult to explain the speed and success with which children acquire language, particularly given the variable nature of the adult speech to which they are exposed. From this, as we will see in Unit 3, many psycholinguists have concluded that children must be born with a genetically transmitted aptitude for language. Questions have been raised about where in the brain this language mechanism is located.

So, by studying the brain, neuropsychologists believe that they can expand our understanding of what language is, our knowledge of how it originated and our views on how it is acquired. Two questions in particular have been raised:

- Are there ways in which the human brain differs physically or in terms of its operations from those of other species – and can they be linked to the possession, use or acquisition of language?
- Is it possible to determine where in the brain language is located?

THE HUMAN BRAIN

EXERCISES

2.1 Let us consider the 'difference' issue first. Examine your own ideas. How do you think the human brain might differ from those of other species?

   (a) Is it larger than those of other species?
   (b) Is it more densely packed with neurons than those of other species?
   (c) Is it larger relative to body weight than those of other species?
   (d) Does it grow faster than other brains?

Check the answers before continuing.

2.2 Here are some physical differences between the human brain and those of other species. Consider how these differences may help human beings to use language.

   (a) The upper surface of the brain, or cortex, is much bigger in human beings. The cortex deals with complicated operations, including finding information that has been stored in memory and making connections between different pieces of information.
   (b) The MOTOR area in the brain controls muscular movement. In human brains, more of this area is given over to the control of the mouth, tongue and lips. **Motor**
   (c) The CEREBELLUM at the base of the brain coordinates muscular movements that have become highly automatic. The human cerebellum is much larger in relation to overall brain size. **Cerebellum**
   (d) Human motor areas exercise much greater control over the larynx, the organ that regulates the passage of air in breathing.

THE HEMISPHERES

The search for language in the brain has especially focused on the fact that the two halves of the brain seem to serve rather different purposes. The human brain (and those of other species) consists of two HEMISPHERES, **Hemispheres** one on the right and one on the left, which are interlinked by a dense

Corpus callosum web of millions of nerves called the CORPUS CALLOSUM. The human
Contralateral brain is CONTRALATERAL. This means that, very broadly, the left hemisphere controls the right side of the body and vice versa. The left
hemisphere tends to be larger than the right.

EXERCISE

2.3 Discuss this in relation to the difference between left-handed and
right-handed people. Then decide:

(a) What would happen to a message that was played to the
right ear?
(b) What would happen to a word that was shown to the left
eye?

In fact, the answer to (b) is a little more complicated than we
have suggested. Check with the answer key.

Early research investigated whether language was processed by one of
the hemispheres rather than the other. One important research method
Dichotic listening used is known as DICHOTIC LISTENING.

A researcher called Kimura (1961) prepared two recordings. Each
recording consisted of three numbers. They were timed so that the
numbers in each recording occurred at exactly equal intervals. Kimura
asked his subjects to put on headphones, and played one set of numbers
to the right ear and one set to the left ear. He then asked them to report
what they had heard. They reported the numbers played to the right ear
much more accurately than the numbers played to the left ear.

EXERCISE

2.4 Study the report of the research. What conclusions do you draw
about which hemisphere is associated with language?

BROCA AND WERNICKE

Many years earlier, the French surgeon Pierre Paul Broca (1824–1880)
had found that, when patients suffered serious damage to a particular

part of the left hemisphere of the brain as the result of an accident or stroke, their language was often seriously affected. Broca studied 20 cases whose speech was impaired. He found that 19 of them had suffered damage to an area (now known as BROCA'S AREA) in front of and just above the left ear. As a result, he later declared: 'Nous parlons avec l'hémisphère gauche' ('We speak with the left hemisphere').

Broca's area

A little later, the German neurologist Carl Wernicke (1848–1904) also studied patients who suffered from APHASIA (loss of language). Wernicke tracked the deficit to damage affecting a different area: one just behind the left ear and now known as WERNICKE'S AREA. But what was quickly evident was that the symptoms that Wernicke described in his patients were very different from those that Broca had described in his.

Aphasia

Wernicke's area

EXERCISE

2.5 Here are examples of the language of patients suffering from Broca's aphasia and from Wernicke's aphasia. In both cases, the patients are describing a picture of a family in a kitchen. In the picture, a mother is washing up at an overflowing sink. She has her back to a boy and girl. The boy has climbed on to a stool and is trying to get some cakes out of a cupboard, but the stool is falling over.

What are the main differences in the language of the patients? (Note: + indicates a pause.)

BROCA'S APHASIA

Ah + ah + girl and boy, ah oh er er dear + girl (*points to the woman*) cof (*points to the cloth*) and er oh er dear me + er (*points to the water*) um steps (*points to the stool*) er steps um window, curtains . . . a pot and an er (*points to water*) oh dear me + OK.

WERNICKE'S APHASIA

Well it's a it's a it's a place and it's a g-girl and a boy + and the-they've got obviously something which is made some made made made well it's just beginning to go and be rather unpleasant (ha! ha!) um and this is in the this is the the woman and she's put putting some stuff and the it's it's that's being

> really too big t-to do and nobody seems to have got anything there at all at all and er it's + I'm rather surprised that but there you are this this er this stuff this is coming they were both being one and another er put here and er um um I suppose the idea is that the er two people should be fairly good but I think it's going somewhere and as I say it's down again.
>
> (Funnell, 1983)

The original accounts of Broca's and Wernicke's aphasia emphasised major differences like those illustrated here. But there is more recent evidence of patients who show a mixture of the two syndromes. So we must be cautious about making generalisations which associate impaired grammar too closely with damage to Broca's area and impaired vocabulary too closely with damage to Wernicke's. It may of course be that the precise location of Broca's area and Wernicke's area varies somewhat from person to person.

LATERALISATION

The findings of Broca and Wernicke led to a view that the left hemisphere was the DOMINANT (i.e. more important) one for language in most people. However, there was also evidence of left-handed people who had right-hemisphere dominance for language.

Dominant

Broca put forward the idea that the two hemispheres might be PLASTIC at birth – i.e. that either might be capable of becoming the dominant one for language. It was later suggested that the process of LATERALISATION, in which language became predominantly located in the left hemisphere, coincided with a CRITICAL PERIOD during which the child was acquiring its first language.

Plastic

Lateralisation
Critical period

This led to interest in cases where the left hemisphere was damaged early in life by an accident or by surgery. Did language relocate itself to the right hemisphere? There was some evidence that this happened if the damage occurred before the age of five.

EXERCISE

2.6 Rasmussen and Milner (1977) examined a large number of subjects (some with early brain damage and some without) to establish which hemisphere was the dominant one for speech.

Figures 2.1 and 2.2 below show their findings in graphic form (N refers to the number of subjects in each group). What do they suggest about:

the relationship between handedness and language?
the effects of early damage to the left hemisphere?

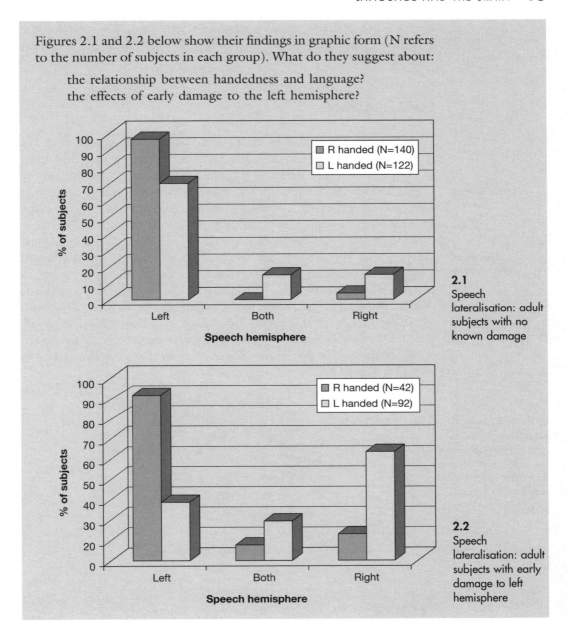

2.1
Speech lateralisation: adult subjects with no known damage

2.2
Speech lateralisation: adult subjects with early damage to left hemisphere

As we have seen, the situation is not entirely clear. Some patients appear to re-lateralise speech after early brain damage while others do not. A lot may depend upon precisely what part of the left hemisphere is damaged.

Recent evidence has cast further doubt on the plasticity theory. It has been found that some young children do not fully recover their language after left-hemisphere damage. Conversely, some people who suffer left-hemisphere damage as adults do go on to re-lateralise language to their right hemisphere.

LOCALISATION

Localisation

While the areas identified by Broca and Wernicke are important in the processing of language, that is not the same as saying that they show us conclusively where language is located in the brain. The question of LOCALISATION has been much investigated. The early findings arose from a precautionary measure adopted by brain surgeons. When surgeons operate on a patient's brain, they try as far as possible to steer clear of any areas that are closely connected with language. To establish where those areas are, they use a technique known as ELECTRICAL STIMULATION in which a mild electric current is administered to exposed areas of the patient's cortex while the patient is under a local anaesthetic. The effect is to briefly disable any language operations that are controlled by the part of the brain to which the current is applied. This has enabled neurosurgeons to link certain aspects of language with certain parts of the brain.

Electrical stimulation

An example of the evidence obtained from electrical stimulation is shown in Figure 2.3.

2.3
Cortical electrical stimulation. Areas of the left hemisphere of the brain that are associated with different language operations: evidence from electrical stimulation (from Deacon, 1997: 290)

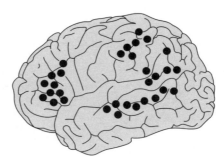

naming, reading, grammar

EXERCISE

2.7 Study Figure 2.3.

(a) What conclusions do you reach about where language is located in the brain?

(b) Can you suggest any reason why the areas identified by Broca and Wernicke might be important to language use – even if they are not where language as a whole is stored?

In addition to the stimulation evidence, modern BRAIN IMAGING **Brain imaging** equipment permits researchers to track activity in the brain in the form of electrical impulses or the movement of blood. The findings from this research confirm the impression that language is widely distributed throughout the brain. What appears to be critical is the way in which the brain is massively interconnected, enabling information to be transmitted very rapidly from one part to another.

THE RIGHT HEMISPHERE

The idea of a language organ localised in the left hemisphere is also challenged by evidence that the right hemisphere contributes much more to language than was previously thought. People who have suffered brain damage to the right hemisphere are usually able to speak and express themselves normally; but they show problems in following narratives and grasping logical connections. What is more, it appears that it is the right hemisphere that processes the PROSODIC features of speech: namely **Prosodic** rhythm and intonation patterns.

EXERCISE

2.8 Consider this evidence from the point of view of a listener.

(a) What is the advantage of processing the sounds of the language with the left hemisphere and the intonation with the right?

(b) What is the advantage of processing grammatical patterns with the left hemisphere and narrative structure with the right?

PROJECT

Test the findings shown in Figure 2.1 above using the dichotic listening method.

Record two pieces from the radio news, read by the same newsreader. Use different cassettes for the two recordings. Put the cassettes into separate players, each with its own earpiece. Ask your subjects to place one earpiece in the right ear and one in the left. Play both recordings simultaneously and at the same volume. Afterwards, ask your subjects to repeat what they heard so that you can establish which piece of news they recall best. Remember that recall of the piece played to the right ear indicates left-hemisphere dominance and vice versa. At the end, ask your subjects whether they are left-handed, right-handed or ambidextrous, and make a note. Use quite a large number of subjects (around 30–40). Analyse the relationship between handedness and hemisphere dominance for language.

LANGUAGE AND THE GRAMMAR GENE

3

If you asked a person in the street how they came to acquire their native language, they would probably tell you that they learnt it somehow from their parents. That is an odd belief. Consider how complex language is. Consider that our parents do not set out with any deliberate intention to teach us.

The question of how we come to acquire language has been an important concern of psycholinguistics from its early days.

BEHAVIOURISM

As we saw in Chapter 1, during the first half of the twentieth century, psychology was dominated by an approach known as behaviourism. Behaviourists regarded the mind as unknowable. Instead of trying to speculate on how human beings think and reason, they believed it was more profitable to study human behaviour. At its most extreme, behaviourism came to suggest that behaviour was entirely the product of external factors – and even to question whether there was such as thing as the mind.

Working within this framework, behaviourist psychologists attempted to account for language acquisition. In his *Verbal Behavior* (1957), B.F. Skinner traced an analogy between the process of acquiring one's first language and a well-known behaviourist experiment in which a pigeon was trained through rewards to play table tennis (or at least to follow some of the rules of the game). He argued that languages were acquired through a process of STIMULUS–RESPONSE–REWARD.

Much of the process of acquiring a language was seen as a question of imitating the language of one's parents. The infant formed associations between words and real-world objects. An object acted as a stimulus

Stimulus–response–reward

and the word that named it was the response that it elicited. By dint of constant repetition, the association became a matter of habit. The infant would receive two types of reward for the correct use of language:

- the infant would get what it wanted (food, drink, comfort);
- the infant would earn its parents' approval.

These rewards would ensure that the infant acquired more and more language. The language would be shaped by adult correction until it became adult-like.

EXERCISE

3.1 What objections can you raise to this theory? You may wish to consider:

(a) whether there is a close analogy between an infant learning a language and a pigeon being trained to play table tennis;

(b) whether stimulus–response–reward is an appropriate explanation of how we learn the names of objects;

(c) whether parents really correct their children;

(d) whether children imitate their parents' speech;

(e) what kind of a model the parents' speech provides.

CHOMSKY'S ARGUMENTS

Noam Chomsky (1959) rebutted Skinner's ideas in a famous review of his book. In the review and in his later writings, he challenged the ideas **Empiricist** of everybody who takes the EMPIRICIST view that children learn their first language from the environment. We will now consider some of the points that Chomsky made.

EXERCISES

3.2 Here are extracts from the language of a child (Sophie) at three different ages. Briefly identify the changes that have occurred. Then consider the changes in relation to the time span.

TWO YEARS FOUR MONTHS (2;4)

Child   daddy come down too
Mother   who's coming down too
Child   daddy
Mother   daddy no where's daddy
Child   me want + daddy come down
Mother   working sweetie

THREE YEARS OLD (3;0)

Child   why did you give her + to her when her been flu
Mother   to cheer her up
Child   what did her have wrong with her
Mother   flu
Child   why + why do + me + why didn't me get flu ever
Mother   I don't know you didn't get it did you that time
Child   why didn't me get flu

THREE YEARS ELEVEN MONTHS (3;11)

Child   um + um + he + he had his own room and + he + he had a pointy thing and a machine you see
Mother   a machine
Child   and + and + he heard he say if you push that button again and the man did and you see and + um + he + and he + all the paper flied outside
Mother   oh because it was a wind machine
Child   yes

(source: Fletcher, 1988)

3.3   Look again at the extracts in 3.2. How often does the mother correct the child? Comment on this in relation to behaviourist theory.

3.4   Now consider this scenario. Child A aged 7 has a low IQ of 70 and has learning difficulties at school. Child B aged 7 has a higher than average IQ of 130 and does well in school tests. Child A has a more limited vocabulary than Child B and does not express himself very well. But both children have mastered the basic grammar of English and rarely produce sentences that are grammatically unacceptable or incomprehensible. What are your comments?

3.5 Recall that behaviourist theory was based upon the idea that a child acquires language by imitating its adult carers. Here is an example of natural adult language. In what ways might it not be a model for a child to imitate?

> *Taxi driver being interviewed:*
> well er depends on what time of day + if if somebody was to jump into my taxi and it was eight o'clock in the evening and + I was just going home + and they said take me to Southampton or Bournemouth and it was erm was a blizzard on and snowing or pouring with rain or heavy fog I would + think twice about going.
>
> (Underwood, 1975)

Chomsky made a number of points supporting his view that an infant could not learn its first language just by listening to the adults around it. They included:

- *Timescale.* In the space of around five years, the child acquires a vocabulary of about 5,000 words and the ability to produce a range of well-formed utterances.
- *Carer correction.* Carers tend to correct facts rather than grammar (though they are more likely to repeat the child's sentences if they are grammatically correct). Any attempts to correct grammar and phonology produce little immediate effect.
- *Intelligence.* All children achieve mastery of their first language regardless of variations in intelligence and in their ability to perform other COGNITIVE (mental) operations. This suggests that language is a faculty that is independent of general thinking skills.

Cognitive

- *Input to the child.* Chomsky (1965) described as 'DEGENERATE' the adult speech from which the child supposedly acquires language. It contains all the features of natural speech (hesitations etc.) – including errors of grammar. The child is exposed to a range of speakers, with different voices and accents. In other words, the child encounters examples of what is often called PERFORMANCE. But what the child has to acquire from this diverse material is COMPETENCE: access to the underlying rules that enable us to produce grammatical sentences.

Degenerate

Performance

Competence

Chomsky argued that possessing a language enables us to produce an infinite number of sentences. If the child simply imitated what it heard, then it would only ever possess a relatively small number. What it needs to do is to internalise a set of language rules so that it can create entirely new sentences – including many *that it has never heard before*.

NATIVISM

Chomsky argued that an infant could not possibly acquire a complex system such as language in such a short time and on the basis of such limited evidence – unless it received some sort of assistance. He concluded that human beings must have a capacity to acquire language which was INNATE (i.e. they were born with it). This view of how we acquire language is known as NATIVISM.

In his early writings, Chomsky envisaged a LANGUAGE ACQUISITION DEVICE which triggered the process of language acquisition. More recently, he has tried to be more specific about precisely what knowledge is transmitted genetically to the infant in order to give it a head start along the road to language. He believes that the infant is born with a UNIVERSAL GRAMMAR (UG) which helps it to recognise the distinctive features that are shared by all languages. From its earliest days, the infant realises that there is something special about the sounds that we call speech. Its innate UG assists it in imposing patterns upon what it hears.

Innate
Nativism
Language acquisition device

Universal grammar

PRINCIPLES AND PARAMETERS

EXERCISE

3.6 Let us look at one of the features (Chomsky calls them PRIN-CIPLES) that all languages are believed to share. Study the following English sentences. Divide each one into groups of words that seem to hang together. Then decide if some of these groups are more important than others.

Principles

(a) My aunt and uncle bought a house with the money.
(b) The old man with the long beard was reading a newspaper.

English, like all known languages, is STRUCTURE DEPENDENT. Its sentences consist of words grouped together into units. The units are hierarchical: some are more fundamental to the sentence than others. An understanding of this characteristic is said to be one of the principles in an infant's UG.

Structure dependent

Although languages share some common features, it is obvious that they also vary greatly in the way they express ideas. Much of what the infant acquires must clearly be specific to its target language.

EXERCISE

3.7 Compare the verb *to speak* in English and Italian. What important differences do you notice?

I speak	parlo
you speak	parli
he/she speaks	parla
we speak	parliamo
you speak	parlate
they speak	parlano

Pro-drop

Some languages use inflections at the end of the verb (*parlo*) to show who or what the subject is. So they do not need to use personal pronouns (*I, you, we, they*). They are known as PRO-DROP languages because they can, if they wish, omit the pronoun. In others, such as English, the pronoun is obligatory. So the infant here faces a two-way choice: to use the pronoun or to drop it.

Parameter

This is what Chomsky calls a PARAMETER. He suggests that UG sensitises the infant to the need to make a choice. When the infant is exposed to its target language, it 'switches' the parameter to 'Pro-drop' or to 'Pronoun' according to the type of language it encounters.

UG thus consists of a set of principles that are common to all languages and a set of parameters that can be adjusted in one of two ways. These give the child a genetic advantage in its task of acquiring the language to which it is exposed.

ORDER OF ACQUISITION

Natural order

Sometimes associated with a nativist view of language acquisition is the theory that all infants acquire the grammatical features of a language in a similar order (sometimes called a NATURAL ORDER). Early language acquisition researchers investigated this theory. Roger Brown (1973) conducted a study using data from three children which suggested that certain grammatical features (inflections and function words like *a* and *of*) were indeed acquired in a fixed sequence. Table 3.1 shows part of the sequence.

Table 3.1 Order of acquisition

Feature	Example	Age
-ing	Mommy driving	1;7–2;4
in, on	Ball in cup, Doggie on sofa	2;3–2;6
-s plural	Kitties eat my ice cream	2;3–2;9
irregular past forms	came, went, sat, broke	2;11–3;10
possessive	Mommy's balloon	2;2–3;4
full form of the verb to be	He is	2;3–3;3
articles: a/the	I see a kitty	2;4–3;10
regular past forms	Mommy pulled the wagon	2;2–4;0
present verbs: 3rd person -s	Kathy hits	2;2–3;10

Source: Brown, 1973

EXERCISE

3.8 (a) How would it support a nativist view of language acquisition if all children were shown to acquire certain features of their language in the same order?

(b) Study the list above and decide what evidence it offers of a natural order of acquisition. Look carefully at the age ranges that are given for each feature.

(c) Do you think that the difficulty of the features might have been a factor or not? What about their frequency?

(d) What do you think the researcher understood by 'acquired'? What criteria would you use to decide if a child had 'acquired' a feature or not?

Many researchers still believe that children acquire certain features of a language in a natural order. But the evidence is not clear-cut and there are uncertainties about the way some of the research has been designed.

PROJECT

Choose some child language data which are LONGITUDINAL – i.e. which track the developing language of a child over a period of time. There is a large database of child language entitled CHILDES (accessible at www.childes.psy.cmu.edu) which is freely available to researchers. If you use one of the files, be sure to acknowledge which corpus you used and include a citation to

Longitudinal

MacWhinney, B. (2000) *The CHILDES Project: Tools for Analyzing Talk*. Mahwah, NJ: Lawrence Erlbaum Associates.

Focus on the language of two or three children. Look for evidence of the child making accurate use of the features in Table 3.1, and note the age at which this first occurs. See if your evidence supports Brown's order of acquisition or not. When you write up your study, be sure to mention any problems you had in ascertaining whether 'acquisition' had or had not occurred.

LANGUAGE AND THE CHILD

4

Unit 3 explored the nativist view that infants are born with a genetically inherited Universal Grammar which gives them a head start in making sense of the adult speech that surrounds them. This is the most influential view of language acquisition; but it is not the only one. There are many researchers who believe that adult language is more informative than Chomsky suggested. There are others who have produced evidence that a child actively forms and tests its own hypotheses based upon the language that it hears. These accounts do not necessarily disprove the nativist case; but they indicate that the idea of an innate language mechanism may not be the only solution to the question of how children acquire language.

In this unit, rather than adult speech in general, we will examine the type of speech that adults use towards children. This is known as CHILD-DIRECTED SPEECH (CDS), though you will also find it called MOTHERESE, BABY TALK and CARER TALK. We will also examine how children react to this input. The evidence will lead us to look critically at three of Chomsky's assertions:

Child-directed speech
Motherese
Baby talk
Carer talk

- that adult speech is 'degenerate';
- that adults do not correct children's speech;
- that language is separate from general thinking skills.

EXERCISE

4.1 Reflect upon your own experience of adults (including yourself) speaking to children.

(a) In what ways do adults modify their language? Make a list in terms of:

PHONOLOGY – GRAMMAR – LEXIS (vocabulary)

(b) In an important early article, Ferguson (1977) suggested that CDS had three important functions:

SIMPLIFYING – CLARIFYING – EXPRESSING (feelings)

Suggest which of these purposes is served by each of the features you have listed.

(c) Finally: do you get the impression that CDS becomes more complex as the child gets older? Or not?

CDS AND SPEECH TO ADULTS

An important research study (Newport *et al.*, 1977) compared CDS with speech that was directed at an adult. The study produced some interesting findings. Table 4.1 shows the differences in sentence structure that were observed. The first figure shows the average length of the **Mean length of** utterances in syllables (the MEAN LENGTH OF UTTERANCE). The other **utterance** figures are percentages of all the utterances that were recorded.

Table 4.1 CDS and adult directed speech compared: syntax

	CDS	Adult-directed speech
Mean length of utterance	4.24	11.94
Grammatically correct whole sentences (%)	60	58
Well-formed isolated phrases (%)	17	9
Declarative sentences (%)	30	87
Questions (%)	44	9
Imperatives (%)	18	2

Source: Newport, Gleitman and Gleitman, 1977

EXERCISE

4.2 (a) Compare child- and adult-directed speech in the first three rows of Table 4.1. What are the differences and what are the similarities?

(b) Does this evidence support Chomsky's view of CDS?

(c) Now compare the percentages of the three types of sentence (declaratives, questions, imperatives). Why do you think they differ between children and adults? Does this assist language acquisition?

(d) Does it help children to recognise sentence patterns if they hear questions like:

Is Daddy reading a book? Have you eaten the biscuits? Did he break a glass?

The CDS was analysed further to see what functions it fulfilled that might assist the language learning process. The most important functions turned out to be:

- DEIXIS (literally 'pointing'): drawing attention to the presence or absence of objects and people.
- REPETITION: repeating the same words or the same idea (*Go find the duck – yes, go find it – the duck – go get the duck*).
- EXPANSION: paraphrasing or adding to what the child said. Example: Child says *allgone Daddy*. Mother says: *yes, Daddy's gone to work.*

Table 4.2 shows the percentage of utterances in CDS that performed these functions; it compares them with the percentages in normal, adult-directed speech.

Table 4.2 CDS and adult directed speech compared: function (%)

	CDS	Adult-directed speech
Deixis	16	2
Repetition	23	0
Expansion	6	0

Source: Newport, Gleitman and Gleitman, 1977

EXERCISE

4.3 Study Table 4.2.

(a) Comment on the differences between CDS and adult-directed speech.

(b) In what ways do you think these three functions might assist the process of language acquisition?

Now here is an example of a conversation between a child and its parents.

1	*Child*	pancakes away + duh duh stomach
2	*Mother*	pancakes away in the stomach yes that's right
3	*Child*	eat apples
4	*Mother*	eating apples on our pancakes aren't we?
5	*Child*	on our pancakes
6	*Mother*	you like apples on your pancakes?
7	*Child*	eating apples + hard
8	*Mother*	what? + hard to do the apples isn't it?

9	*Child*	more pancakes?
10	*Father*	you want more pancakes?
11	*Child*	those are daddy's
12	*Father*	daddy's gonna have his pancakes now
13	*Child*	ne ne one a daddy's + ne ne one in plate + right there
14	*Father*	you want some more on your plate?

(Snow, 1986)

EXERCISE

4.4   Study the conversation.

Turns

    (a) Comment on the adult TURNS. Are they potentially helpful to language acquisition?

    (b) Comment on how the child reacts.

    (c) What evidence is there that the adults are trying to speak at the same level as the child?

Scaffolding   This kind of support is termed SCAFFOLDING. Chomsky was correct in maintaining that carers do not often correct a child's language. But they frequently try to make sense of what the child is saying, and, wherever possible, treat the child's utterances as if they were part of a normal **Recast** conversation. They frequently RECAST what the child says, and thus:

- indirectly correct it;
- provide a model of what the child intended to say;
- introduce vocabulary that the child has not yet acquired.

So, contrary to what Chomsky implied, the child does get a lot of feedback.

THE PHONOLOGY OF CDS

One of the most striking features of CDS is the way in which adults adapt their normal phonological patterns. Compared with adult-directed speech, CDS is marked by:

- a high pitch level;
- a slower speech rate;
- more pausing (usually at clause boundaries);
- heavy stress (marked by steep pitch patterns) on the most important words;
- lengthening of the last syllable in a clause.

EXERCISE

4.5 (a) Consider this hypothetical transcription of an utterance reported by Foster-Cohen (1999: 63). In what way might the features described above help the child to identify important units of vocabulary and grammar?

> YougotoutoftheBEDintheN-I-G-H-T + didyou +
> andranaROUNDintheD-A-R-K+ +
> thatsoundsaDAFTthingtoD-O

CAPITALS = stressed word   + = pause
- = a lengthened syllable

(b) Can you suggest any reason why adults use a high pitch level when speaking to a child?

BOOTSTRAPPING

In looking at the phonology of CDS, an intriguing question has arisen: how does the child manage to recognise individual units of language within the chunks of connected speech that it hears? There is no system of pauses between words in speech as there is in writing. A pre-linguistic child simply hears stretches of continuous sound. It has no vocabulary that would enable it to break these chunks into the smaller units that we call words.

EXERCISE

4.6 Suggest how children come to recognise that an utterance consists of a series of moveable units which are likely to recur in other utterances. You may wish to think of your own experience of listening to a foreign language.

One solution is to assume that UG provides them in advance with an innate knowledge of the word as a unit of meaning. That may or may not be the case; but it still does not explain how children come to *recognise* words. There is much evidence that they use their own problem-solving techniques.

They start by identifying in continuous speech some of the words that they have heard in isolation. However, this only works for a limited number of words – mainly names. Therefore, they focus instead on whole chunks of language that recur in the speech they have heard. One result is that they produce grammatically incorrect utterances which they have never heard adults make: for example (Peters, 1983): *What he wants? Why you can't open it? What his name is?* Here, the child seems to have adopted chunks of language from indirect speech (I wonder *what he wants*, I don't know *why you can't open it*, Do you know *what his name is?*).

They gradually begin to break the chunks into smaller pieces. In doing so, they seem to apply systematic techniques – sometimes techniques specific to the language they are acquiring. This phenomenon is known **Bootstrapping** as BOOTSTRAPPING.

EXERCISE

4.7 Researchers have pointed out that children acquiring English often produce the following versions of the three words GIRAFFE, MONKEY and BANANA:

GIRAFFE → raffe   MONKEY → monkey   BANANA → nana

Say the words aloud and see if you can work out what bootstrapping strategy the children are using in order to identify the words. Remember that they have to segment them out of longer utterances: *Can you see the giraffe/monkey/banana in the picture?*

This is an example of rhythm being used for bootstrapping. Children are born with a natural sense of rhythm. They come to recognise that English has a tendency to a basic strong-weak pattern, as in words like *PAper, FORty, PHOtoGRAphic*. They then work out that it is a good strategy to operate on the assumption that words begin with a strong syllable (in fact, most do). So when they hear *CanyouseethegiRAFFE*, they assume that a boundary falls before RAFFE. Children also combine words mistakenly as in *I like-it the elephant*, where LIKE-IT, frequently overheard in speech, is taken to be a single strong-weak word.

EXERCISE

4.8 Using a rhythmic bootstrapping technique, what version would an infant produce of the words:

baboon – camel – rhinoceros – gorilla – elephant – hippopotamus – mosquito – porcupine?

Another type of bootstrapping technique may assist children in recognising inflections and grammatical patterns. This is known as SYNTACTIC BOOTSTRAPPING.

Syntactic bootstrapping

Early language acquisition experiments used invented words to test whether very young children understood the differences between various types of noun. Shown a picture of an imaginary animal and told *It's a wug*, children of only 17 months proved capable of constructing a plural (*They're wugs*) in order to describe a picture of two of the creatures. Children of this age discriminated similarly between *It's a sib*, used to refer to a picture of something that was clearly COUNTABLE and *It's sib*, used to refer to something that was not. They also recognised that *It's Dax* potentially featured a name (a PROPER NOUN) while *It's a dax* featured a common noun.

Countable

Proper noun

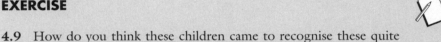

EXERCISE

4.9 How do you think these children came to recognise these quite abstract areas of grammar? They obviously could not have explained the rules.

Evidence of bootstrapping suggests that children actively use their intelligence in order to puzzle out where word boundaries fall and to identify grammatical categories. It is possible that all human beings are cognitively disposed (even from a very early age) to trace patterns in material that appears at first to be shapeless. This view of language acquisition seems to have brought us quite a long way from Chomsky's view that language is not dependent upon other cognitive processes.

PROJECT

Collect your own samples of child-directed speech and of the responses of the infant. Study a younger brother or sister or the young child of a neighbour or relative. Ideally, choose an infant of around 2.5–3 years old. Record the conversations between the child and its carers on a regular basis (say, for half an hour once every week). An alternative might be to record conversations between a child and its older siblings; this is a type of CDS about which we have little evidence.

As you collect your data, identify any interesting sections and transcribe them. When you feel that you have enough data, analyse them to find out (for example):

- What evidence is there of scaffolding by the carers? How often does it happen?
- What evidence is there of the three functions identified by Newport *et al.* (deixis, repetition and expansion)?
- To what extent do the carers use unusual phonology in their CDS?
- What evidence is there of the child making use of rhythm for bootstrapping? Does he/she seem to focus on parts of words that are more prominent and easier to hear?

LANGUAGE AND DISADVANTAGE

5

The title of this unit really covers two different areas:

1 How 'EXCEPTIONAL CIRCUMSTANCES' in childhood might affect the way in which a child's language develops. This is especially of interest to those psycholinguists who want to establish whether language is indeed innate. If it is, outside circumstances should have little or no effect on the way that language develops.

Exceptional circumstances

2 What happens when language goes wrong. Psycholinguists have two agendas here. By discovering more about the processes underlying language disability, they can provide insights for therapists, clinicians and others who help sufferers. They can also gain possible insights into how language operates in normal circumstances. Here, a distinction is made between:

- language problems which are ACQUIRED: affecting the sufferer after first language competence has been established;

Acquired

- language problems which are DEVELOPMENTAL: affecting the speed or the completeness of first language acquisition.

Developmental

Within the category of developmental problems, we can distinguish at least two different areas of research (though the two sometimes overlap):

(a) language impairment: the effects of certain syndromes like AUTISM on how a child uses language;

Autism

(b) gaps in competence: problems in certain areas of language manifested by children who are otherwise developing normally.

EXERCISE

5.1 Decide which of the above terms best describes the following:

aphasia after an accident; language acquisition by a deaf child; autism; the language of twins; stuttering; the effects of a stroke; dyslexia; Downs Syndrome; depriving a young child of language

We first examine a condition where otherwise normal children have problems with a single area of language competence.

DYSLEXIA

Dysgraphia Children who show signs of developmental dyslexia are slower than usual to acquire reading skills, or they employ reading processes that are different from those adopted by most children. Many dyslexics also experience *writing* problems, technically known as DYSGRAPHIA. We consider these writing problems first.

EXERCISE

5.2 Miles (1993) identifies 13 spelling problems which dyslexics have. Here are examples of seven of the types. Describe these seven types of error.

1	get → cet	5	squeezing → scweecing
2	oxygen → oschun	6	daddy → baddy
3	else → esle	7	language → languaguage
4	father → fther		

Sounded letter Now match each example to one of these descriptions (a SOUNDED LETTER is one where the letter corresponds to a sound in the pronunciation).

A   duplication of one or more sounded letters
B   syllable missed out
C   b–d confusion
D   a sounded letter missed out
E   attempt to write the sound(s) phonetically
F   misrepresentation (mishearing?) of the sound
G   mistaken letter order

Now classify each of the errors in Table 5.1 as one of the seven types.

Table 5.1 Spellings of various dyslexic subjects

Target	Spelling	Target	Spelling	Target	Spelling
first	firsk	because	deakos	ropes	roaps
exceptionally	explunaly	people	pepeole	damage	damageage
odd numbers	obd nudners	baby	baybiy	suddenly	suddly
departure	depacher	pudding	pubbing	forty	fortyty
army	amry	different	diffent	examined	igzamind
negotiations	nocosiatios	square	sqaurare	two	tow

Source: Miles, 1993

In order to read or write successfully, a child needs to be able to establish a link between the sounds of the language and the way words are spelt. In some cases of dysgraphia, the problems seem to be phonological – reflecting the way in which the writer hears the sounds of the language. In others, they seem to be visual – reflecting the way in which the writer visualises the written form of the word.

EXERCISE

5.3 Look at the examples you have just studied. Which types of spelling problem (A to G) suggest that the writer has problems with the sounds of the words and which appear to show that the writer has problems in remembering the form of the words? Which group suggests that the writer has a clear idea of the sound–spelling relationship but is not using it accurately in working out how to spell words?

In order to understand dyslexia, we need to know a little about normal reading processes. One theory has it that we use two distinct routes in reading. The LEXICAL route, especially important with spelling systems like the English one, involves recognising words as a whole. That is the only way that a reader can master irregular words such as YACHT. But we also need a second, SUB-LEXICAL, route if we are to work out how to say unfamiliar words: for example, names that we have not met before or words that we have only ever heard spoken. This route enables the reader to use sound–spelling rules to work out the pronunciation of a

Lexical

Sub-lexical

word from its letters. In this way, you could work out how to say non-words such as SWILK or GLECT.

When dyslexics are tested, some show difficulties in working out how to pronounce non-words. The problem may derive from their inability to divide words into their constituent sounds: for example, to say which word is left when we take the /s/ out of /best/. This group is said to suffer from PHONOLOGICAL DYSLEXIA; as we have seen, difficulties in distinguishing sounds can affect their writing, too.

Phonological dyslexia

Others can pronounce non-words but find it hard to recognise words like GAUGE or YACHT which are irregular. They might also pronounce a word like PINT as if it rhymed with MINT and HINT. This group is said to suffer from SURFACE DYSLEXIA. It is these dyslexics who may have problems in remembering the *forms* of words when they come to write. Their phonological knowledge is often sound, so they might try to spell words as they are said: they might write EXCEPT as *iksept*.

Surface dyslexia

The two-way divide that has been described is rather a simplification (and, indeed, some specialists disagree with it). Many dyslexics show signs of both types of deficit, but to different degrees. Reading and writing can also be affected to different degrees, though writing often suffers more than reading.

EXERCISE

5.4 Diagnose these problems of dyslexia and dysgraphia:

Subject A can read the word INLAND but has problems with ISLAND.

Subject B wrote BISCUIT as *bisket* and NEPHEW as *neffue*.

Subject C read the non-word COBE as *comb* and PLOON as *spoon*.

Subject D spelt EMPTY as *epmty*.

Subject E read BIND as *binned* and SCENE as *sken*.

Subject F could not write down the non-word SPID.

Subject G read STOVE as *stuv*.

Subject H read QUAY as *quay* but read the name WIMPOLE as *winkle*.

Subject I wrote Please <u>right</u> down what you have for <u>sail</u>.

(Adapted from Ellis, 1993)

LANGUAGE DEPRIVATION

Let us now look at a very different situation: an example of 'exceptional circumstances'.

In 1967 a researcher called Lenneberg suggested that there was a CRITICAL PERIOD for a child to acquire its first language. If, for any reason, the child was prevented from doing so, it would not go on to achieve full linguistic competence. Lenneberg suggested that the critical period might coincide with the stage during which language became LATERALISED in one hemisphere of the brain (see Unit 2).

Critical period

Lateralised

One problem is that there is considerable disagreement about precisely when the period ends. Originally, it was said to be at the age of five, when language supposedly became lateralised in the left hemisphere. But many subsequent accounts have assumed that the end of the critical period coincides with adolescence.

The 'critical period' hypothesis has led to interest in those rare cases of children who are deprived of language in the early years of their lives. They fall into two types. There are WOLF CHILDREN who have been found living in the wild like animals; and there are ATTIC CHILDREN who have been kept in seclusion as a result of adult cruelty. We will look at a case of the latter.

Wolf children
Attic children

Susan was the daughter of a Los Angeles man who hated children and felt threatened by the outside world. She was not a healthy child, and at one point there was a suggestion that she might have learning problems. From the age of one, she was tied up on a potty in a small room at the back of the family home. Nobody spoke to her and human contact was limited to feeding.

Susan's mother finally rescued her when she was thirteen. She was taken to a children's hospital, where her progress was monitored by psychologists. They called her 'Genie', the name by which she has since become known. Genie could only understand a few words, and produced only limited phrases such as *stopit* and *nomore*. The question was whether, at the age of thirteen, she could acquire a full language competence.

Once she was put into foster care, Genie began, first slowly then very rapidly, to acquire vocabulary. It did not resemble the basic vocabulary acquired by infants, and included many quite advanced words. Genie began to talk about her terrible experiences during the period before she had had language – indicating that thought and memory are not dependent upon the possession of words. Here is an example of one of her utterances:

> Father hit arm. Big wood. Genie cry . . . Not spit. Father. . . . Father hit big stick. Father is angry. Father hit Genie big stick. Father take piece wood hit. Father make me cry. Father is dead.
>
> (Curtiss, 1977: 35)

EXERCISE

5.5 Examine Genie's vocabulary and syntax. What are your conclusions?

Though Genie acquired quite a large vocabulary over the next few years, she seemed to find speech effortful, and her syntax failed to develop. On the other hand, she managed to communicate her basic wishes and needs and was able to construct sentences of her own. In other areas, she seemed to make good cognitive progress, and her mental age increased by a year for every year she was free. However, the possibility was raised that the left hemisphere of her brain had suffered some damage during her period of confinement.

When Genie was eighteen, there was a tussle over custody. In the consequent insecurity, her linguistic development stopped and she even retreated into silence. She is now in an adult home.

EXERCISE

5.6 You now have the facts about Genie.

(a) To what extent does the example of Genie seem to support the idea of a critical period for acquiring a language?

(b) Are there ways in which the case is not entirely clear?

(c) Consider the example of Genie in relation to Chomsky's view that language is a separate faculty from general cognition.

MODULARITY

Let us consider again the question of the relationship between language and our other mental faculties. Chomsky claims that language is a separate component of the mind, on the grounds that, regardless of intelligence, almost every child acquires a full grammatical competence

Modular in its first language. His claim is that language is MODULAR: an independent and self-contained faculty. So are there specific cases which appear to demonstrate this thesis: cases where language is impaired but cognition is not – or vice versa?

EXERCISE

5.7 Which of the following seem to support the idea of a separation between language and other mental capacities? Which seem to contradict it? Which are unclear?

- Sufferers from DOWNS SYNDROME show signs of mental impairment. Their language is also impaired. **Downs Syndrome**

- Children who suffer from WILLIAMS SYNDROME show signs of mental impairment, including low IQs. But they are highly communicative and their language competence appears to be relatively unaffected. **Williams Syndrome**

- Children suffering from AUTISM may be mute until the age of 5, or may do little more than echo the words that adults say to them. Autistic children tend to have very low IQs and may show signs of delayed cognitive as well as linguistic development. They may excel in one or two isolated skills such as painting or music. **Autism**

- SAVANTS are individuals who are severely mentally impaired, but show exceptional gifts, usually in relation to painting and music. Christopher is one such individual. He was diagnosed as brain-damaged early in life and has to live in care. Yet he is able to translate from, and communicate in, some 16 languages. **Savants**

- Those who suffer from SPECIFIC LANGUAGE IMPAIRMENT (SLI) show a language competence that appears to be incomplete: they sometimes have restricted vocabularies and their grammar often lacks inflections and function words. But these individuals do not appear to be mentally impaired in other ways. SLI appears to be inherited genetically. One explanation is that it is the result of acquiring every word as a separate item instead of recognising that there are general rules for producing plurals etc. Another is that SLI sufferers do not hear the inflections at the end of English words. **Specific Language Impairment**

PROJECT

Contact a unit in your college or neighbourhood which provides support for dyslexia. With the permission of the director:

(a)   Interview one or more of the teachers to discover which are the most common reading or writing problems they have observed. Ask also about the kinds of technique that they use to counteract dyslexia.

(b)   Interview one or more of their students to establish what they perceive to be their most common problems.

(c)   Examine the writing or record the reading aloud of one or more of the dyslexic students and analyse the difficulties that occur.

Make sure you obtain the written consent of any students whose work you study. If they are under 16, you should also obtain the consent of their parents.

STORING WORDS

6

Units 6 and 7 focus on vocabulary. They consider these questions:

- What words and parts of words do we store in our mental dictionary?
- What information do we need in order to use a word?
- How are words linked to each other?
- How do we find a word when we need it?

LEXICAL ENTRIES

Somewhere in a language user's mind, there is a store of all the words that they know. This mental dictionary (known as a LEXICON) must contain a reference or LEXICAL ENTRY for every item of vocabulary that they use in their own speech or understand in the speech of others. Obviously, lexicons vary from person to person. Some have a large number of lexical entries; others have fewer. Some people have very specific entries for certain items of vocabulary, while others make do with a general representation. The word ROSE will have much more precise associations in the lexicon of a gardener than in that of a non-gardener.

Lexicon

Lexical entry

Most lexical entries correspond to words such as TABLE – JUMP – HAPPY – ABROAD. These are known as CONTENT WORDS because they have lexical meaning: the kind of meaning that could be given in a dictionary. But what about FUNCTION WORDS like OF – THE – DO (in *Do you like?*) which play a grammatical role rather than bearing meaning? It is often suggested that they form part of a separate store from the main lexicon. When we hear these words, we do not need to seek out a meaning for them, but can just identify them by a simple matching process.

Content words

Function words

EXERCISE

6.1 Which of the following do you think have lexical meaning? Which do not? Which seem to fall somewhere in between?

DRIVE	FATHER	A	TO (to go)	SLOW	IN
MUST	BUT	NEVER	BELONG	FIGHT	IT
NASTY	SUGAR	MICHAEL	WHEN	SO	
LONDON	BEHIND	THAT			

So it is not always easy to say whether a word is represented within the main lexicon. Here is a second issue: what happens when an item of vocabulary consists of two or more words?

EXERCISES

6.2 Suggest how these multi-word items are represented in the lexicon:

IN FRONT OF   INSIDE OUT   THE DAY AFTER TOMORROW

Remember that in other languages, the same ideas might be represented by a single word.

Collocation 6.3 Would you apply the same solution to COLLOCATION? This is a relationship that happens not when words are combined to form a larger expression, but when they often occur together. For example, if you want to talk about somebody who smokes a lot, you do not refer to a *big smoker* or a *great smoker* but to a HEAVY SMOKER. How do you think the lexicon stores the relationship between SMOKER and HEAVY; SPEND and TIME; DRIVE and CAR?

Here is a further question. The word SMOKER is derived from another word by a regular rule:

(to) SMOKE → SMOKER   (to) TEACH → TEACHER
(to) SWIM → SWIMMER

So does SMOKER have an entry of its own or do we assemble it from its two parts when we want to use it?

Units like -ER which can be added to existing words fall into two different types. First of all there are INFLECTIONS, which show the grammatical function of a word in a sentence:

Inflections

WALK → WALKED   WALK → WALKING   WALK → (he) WALKS

In English, inflections are always SUFFIXES, placed at the end of the word.

Suffixes

EXERCISE

6.4 Which do you think is more likely (and more efficient)?

(a) There are separate lexical entries for WALK, WALKED, WALKING etc.

(b) There is one lexical entry for WALK which includes information about how to form WALKED, WALKING etc.

Now here is a rather different case. We sometimes add prefixes or suffixes in order to create new words:

HAPPY → UNHAPPY   HAPPY → HAPPINESS

EXERCISES

6.5 Which do you think is more likely (and more efficient)?

(a) There are separate lexical entries for HAPPY, UNHAPPY, UNHAPPINESS.

(b) There is one lexical entry for HAPPY and others for UN- and -NESS.

6.6 If (b) is the case, then how do we locate the opposites of:

HONEST – UNDERSTAND – MOTIVATE?

(Hint: think of the solution for collocation)

Researchers disagree about whether there are separate lexical entries for these DERIVATIONAL prefixes and suffixes. Recent evidence seems to

Derivational

have moved the discussion in favour of the idea. This would mean that, when a speaker wants to use the word UNHAPPY, they assemble it from its two parts.

All very well, but what about the listener? Remember that the meaning of UNHAPPY is stored in two entries. So in order to understand the word, the listener would have first to take off any prefix (an operation known as PREFIX STRIPPING).

Prefix stripping

EXERCISE

6.7 (a) Describe the prefix-stripping that would take place when somebody heard:

UNCERTAIN, DISAPPEAR, MISMANAGE, INEFFICIENT

(b) Now describe what would happen when somebody heard:

UNDERSTAND, DISAPPOINT, MISTAKE, INFORM

There is a problem here. Some words can be split while others, with similar first syllables, cannot.

EXERCISE

6.8 Consider the following words. Which might possibly be assembled from two lexical entries and which might not?

RENAME   REVISE   RECONSIDER   RETURN   REFRESH
RECOVER   REWRITE   REPLY   REPAIR   REBUILD
RENEW   REMIND   REPRINT

In some cases, the first syllable of a word is clearly a prefix, in others it is not. One solution is to assume that certain words are stored in two parts and others as wholes. But this does not resolve the problem of the listener. Listeners try to match words to lexical entries *as they are hearing them*. So if a listener heard the word DISGUST, he/she would automatically strip off the DIS- and would then have to put it back again:

DISGUST → DIS + GUST → no word GUST → look for DISGUST

Not an efficient process – and one reason why some psycholinguists oppose the idea that prefixes have separate lexical entries.

STORED INFORMATION

Let us leave the vexed question of what are or are not lexical entries. We now consider what information we need to have about a word if we are to use it successfully.

EXERCISE

6.9 Consider this situation.

(a) You want to write the word WRITE.

(b) You want to refer to something that happened yesterday.

(c) You want to be sure that WRITE is the most appropriate word (rather than INSCRIBE or SCRIBBLE or TYPE).

(d) You want to use WRITE in a sentence.

What information do you need about WRITE in order to do this?

A lexical entry is said to fall into two parts. One tells us about the *form of a word*. It includes information on:

- the spelling of the word;
- the pronunciation of the word;
- the MORPHOLOGY of the word, i.e. the way in which it inflects: **Morphology** *WRITE – wrote – written.*

The second part (called the LEMMA) tells us about meaning. It **Lemma** includes:

- the core meaning of the word ('put words on a piece of paper');
- information about how the word differs from others with a similar meaning.

It also contains syntactic knowledge about the word. This may seem strange since the lemma is concerned with meaning. But in order to use the word meaningfully in a sentence we need to know its WORD-CLASS **Word-class** (noun, verb, adjective). WRITE is a verb and likely to come after the subject of the sentence.

EXERCISE

6.10 What would be contained in a lexical entry for these words?

(a) afraid
(b) show
(c) put

WORD MEANING

Let us look more closely at the kind of information on meaning that a lexical entry has to contain.

EXERCISE

6.11 (a) Think of a definition for the word HOUSE.
(b) Compare the word to BUNGALOW, COTTAGE, MANSION. Compare it to APARTMENT.

Category

A noun like HOUSE is best regarded not as 'the name of a person or thing' but as a word that refers to a *class of objects*. Several different types of object might fall into a CATEGORY of this kind: in our example, bungalows, cottages and mansions. In addition, there might be other categories, such as APARTMENT, which do not overlap with it in any way but stand in contrast to it. We understand the limits of the meaning of HOUSE if we know that we have a separate and contrasted word for a living unit that occupies a single floor of a larger building.

If we are able to attach word labels to objects in the real world it is very much because we have learnt to group those objects into categories. Thus, cottages, bungalows and mansions fall into the category HOUSE but apartments do not. So what form do these categories take in our minds? How are we able to identify a two-bedroomed terraced town house as part of the same category as a six-bedroomed farmhouse?

EXERCISE

6.12 Study the following list of words and number them from 1 to 16. Put 1 against the one that you think of as the most typical form of furniture and continue until 16, which is for the least typical. Then compare your answers with those of other students.

carpet	computer	bed	mirror
television	clock	wardrobe	plant stand
table	vase	radiator	curtains
lamp	bookshelf	armchair	cooker

You will probably have found striking similarities in the choices you made. An experiment of this kind by Eleanor Rosch in the 1970s formed the basis for what is known as PROTOTYPE THEORY. It suggests that language users construct a category like FURNITURE, BIRD or VEGETABLE around a central example which is highly typical of the category as a whole. We can then recognise which other objects fall within the category by comparing them to this example. Some will be good examples of the category because they will resemble the PROTO-TYPE quite closely; others will be less good examples; others will clearly not fall into the category at all.

Prototype theory

Prototype

EXERCISE

6.13 One way of explaining this prototype effect is to say that the prototype has all or most of the characteristics that we associate with a particular category while 'less good' members of the category have fewer of those features.

What features do you associate with the category BIRD? Try to think of at least six. Now classify these creatures according to how many of the features each one has. Which ones do you think are closest to the prototype? Which are furthest?

HAWK   SPARROW   OSTRICH   PARROT   THRUSH
DUCK   PENGUIN   BAT   CANARY   OWL

The defining characteristics seem to work for some categories. But not for the category VEGETABLE. In the original experiment, PEA was listed as the prototypical vegetable for Rosch's North American subjects. But CARROT came very near the top.

EXERCISE

6.14 Can you suggest any reasons for this? How different do you think the result might have been if Rosch had conducted her experiment in another country?

PROJECT

Replicate Rosch's experiment. Draw up a list of 25 examples of three or four categories. Ask subjects to number them according to how good an example they are of the category. Examine how consistent their answers are; then try to provide your own explanations for this consistency. You may want to extend Rosch's original experiment by setting the task to subjects of

(a) different ages;
(b) different social backgrounds;
(c) different parts of the country.

You may want to make use of the explanation that Rosch gave to her subjects when preparing them for the task:

> Close your eyes and imagine a true red. Now imagine an orangeish red . . . imagine a purple red. Although you might still name the orange red or the purple red with the term RED, they are not such good examples of RED . . . . Notice that this kind of judgement has nothing to do with how well you like the thing; you can like a purple red better than a true red but still recognise that the colour you like is not a true red.
>
> (Rosch, 1975: 198)

FINDING WORDS

7

In this unit, we consider how we find (RETRIEVE) words when we have need of them. There will be some overlap with Unit 6 since the way in which we store words often assists us in finding them.

Retrieve

LEXICAL ACCESS

There are two aspects of the retrieval process:

- *recognition*: making a match;
- *access*: drawing upon stored information about the word.

A reader has to match the sight of the word on the page with a stored REPRESENTATION of what the word looks like. The result of the matching process is to 'unlock' information in the lexical entry about the word's morphology, its word-class and its meaning.

Representation

EXERCISE

7.1 Now compare the process of retrieving a word when you are:

(a) a listener
(b) a writer
(c) a speaker

Consider whether you are trying to match a particular *form* or a particular *meaning* to a word in your lexicon. Consider what information about the word you would then need to access.

GIVEN A MEANING, FIND A FORM

With speakers and writers, the search is driven by a meaning for which they need to find a word. They are assisted by the fact that words in the same category are grouped together in the mind. There are links between (say) PEAR, APPLE and GRAPE or COW, HORSE and DOG. These **Lexical sets** groups are known as LEXICAL SETS.

EXERCISE

7.2 Suggest what lexical sets these words might be stored in. Then suggest other members of each set.

SPINACH   HAMMER   to MARCH   CUPBOARD
TAXI   HUGE   to FETCH   COAT

We have assumed that writers and speakers identify a word entirely by its meaning. But the process is a little more complex than that.

EXERCISE

7.3 Here are some word meanings in the form of definitions. Find the appropriate words – or at least make an approximate guess at what each word is:

(a) a tropical insect like a cricket that makes a whirring noise, especially in hot weather;
(b) a large enclosed space for keeping birds in;
(c) describes an apparent illness that is all in the mind of the sufferer;
(d) to ignore somebody and refuse to have any dealings with them;
(e) an idea that has been said so often that it is completely unoriginal;
(f) do damage to a holy place;
(g) a small craft which can go under water;
(h) a type of lorry that bends when it turns corners;
(i) a twisted plant that grows in tropical swamps.

Were any of the words difficult to find? Discuss your experience of retrieving them. If you made a guess, how close was it to the target word?

The words in Exercise 7.3 were not very common ones and you may not have known all of them. Where you did know the word, you may have retrieved it easily; but sometimes you may have found yourself in what is called a TIP OF THE TONGUE state. In this, we appear to have some kind of ACCESS CODE – a way of locating a word that is almost like a shape in the mind. It tells us that the word exists. It may also give some clues as to the word's form – perhaps the first syllable. This suggests that we do use form as well as meaning when we look for words, though obviously meaning is what drives the process.

Tip of the tongue
Access code

EXERCISE

7.4 Imagine that you are looking for a word for the railing that runs up alongside a staircase.

(a) You start out with the meaning. Which lexical set would the word fall in?

(b) When you locate the word, what information do you need about it in order to use it in a sentence?

(c) You produce the word BARRIER. It isn't quite the word that you intended. Why did you choose it by mistake?

Further evidence that words in the lexicon are linked by form comes from the mistakes that speakers make. If somebody says BARRIER when they mean BANNISTER, it shows that their search was directed by a general meaning (railings) and a lexical set (architectural features) – but that they also had cues about form which suggested that the target word begins with BA- and ends with -ER.

Mistakes like this provide important insights into the process that is involved in finding a word. They tell us what cues the speaker was following – cues that lead to the wrong word as well as the right one.

EXERCISE

7.5 Here are some examples of actual speaker errors – known as SLIPS OF THE TONGUE. Compare the target words (capitals) with the words that the speaker actually used (italics). What cues to word form were the speakers using? Look not just at the sounds of the words, but also at their length and rhythm.

Slips of the tongue

(a) SYLLABLES → *cylinders*   PROTESTANT → *prostitute*

(b) CONCUBINE → *porcupine*   UNANIMOUSLY →
                                                anonymously

(c) ANTIDOTE → *anecdote*   DETERRENT → *detergent*

(d) OBSOLETE → *absolute*

Here is a further example:

(e) My data consist moanly – maistly . . .

(Fromkin, 1973; Aitchison and Straf, 1982)

What has gone wrong here? And what cues to form does the speaker seem to be following?

GIVEN A FORM, FIND A MEANING

Links between words that have similar forms especially help listeners and readers. Their point of departure is a word form that they have heard in speech or seen on the page. Their first task is to match this form to a representation in their mind:

Phonological representation

- a PHONOLOGICAL REPRESENTATION for a listener;

Written representation

- a WRITTEN REPRESENTATION for a reader.

Let us consider one theory of what happens when listeners try to match words.

On-line

Listening appears to take place ON-LINE: we analyse what a speaker

Cohort theory

is saying while they are still saying it. COHORT THEORY attempts to explain the process.

EXERCISE

7.6 (a) You hear a speaker say the first syllable of a word. It is /saɪ/ (*SY*). Make a list of all the words you can think of that might fit this.

(b) Now you hear a /k/, making /saɪk/ (*SYKE*). Cross off any words from the list that no longer fit the evidence. Which have you kept?

(c) The next sounds are /ɒl/, making /saɪˈkɒl/ (*SYKOL*). Have you now reduced the set of possible matches to one? What is it?

When listeners hear the first part of a word (say, the first syllable), Cohort Theory suggests that they open up a whole group of words (a 'cohort'); these words form possible matches because they begin with the same sounds. As the speaker continues to say the word, the group is gradually narrowed down until there is only one possible match. The word is said to have reached a UNIQUENESS POINT.

Uniqueness point

EXERCISE

7.7 Consider how Cohort Theory would or would not cope with the following spoken words. It may help if you read them aloud.

(a) reading   entertain   unity
(b) sent a page   the way to cut it
(c) a shigarette (speaker who has spent too long in a bar).

In fact, Cohort Theory has now been revised to take account of the 'shigarette' problem. Instead of demanding an exact 100 per cent match, it assumes that the listener will make the 'best fit' to what was heard.

ACTIVATION

Other theories of listening and reading also assume that we start by making a number of possible word matches and then narrow them down to one. This is explained in terms of ACTIVATION. Think of activation as a kind of electric current and all the lexical entries in the lexicon as thousands of tiny light bulbs. If there is a small amount of evidence for a word, the word's bulb lights up dimly; if there is a lot, it lights up very brightly. The possible word matches are said to be in COMPETITION with each other, until finally one bulb becomes so glaringly bright that it wins through and is identified as the correct match.

Activation

Competition

EXERCISE

7.8 Imagine you read the following letters at the end of a line of text:

PROFESS-

Which of the lexical entries below will receive strong activation? Which will receive weak activation? Which will receive no activation – perhaps negative activation? Suggest why.

PROWESS	PROMISE	FOREST	PROFESSOR
MAXIMUM	CONFESSION	PROGRESS	PROFESSION
BALANCE	PREFERS	PROCESSOR	

FREQUENCY

So far, we have discussed the search for words as if it treated all words equally. But are some favoured over others?

EXERCISE

7.9 Here is a group of words that are all superficially similar in that they all have six letters. Would you expect a reader to take the same time to recognise each of the words? If not, which ones would be most readily recognised and why?

INCITE	INCOME	INDEED	INDUCE	INFECT	INFANT
INFAMY	INFIRM	INFORM	INJECT	INJURE	INLAND
INMATE	INSANE	INROAD	INSECT	INSERT	INSIDE
INSIST	INSULT	INTACT	INTEND	INVADE	INVEST
INVENT	INVITE	INVOKE			

Frequency effect   The FREQUENCY EFFECT that we have just encountered can also be explained in terms of activation. One solution is to say that activation flows more quickly to a word that is frequent – because it has flowed in that direction so many times before. It has, in effect, worn a path.

SPREADING ACTIVATION

A similar explanation accounts for another finding. Once you have read a word, it is easier to recognise other words that are closely associated with it. For example, if you read the word PLANE, you are likely to recognise the words *airport*, *pilot*, *runway* and *flight* more quickly than you would do normally – provided they occur quite soon after PLANE. **Prime**   The word PLANE is said to PRIME the others. Again, we might represent this effect in terms of activation flowing along well travelled **Spreading activation**   connections between words – hence the term SPREADING ACTIVATION.

The examples given are of words that fall within the same lexical set as PLANE. But priming effects are also found with other connections between words (for example, collocations, opposites, etc.). We can picture the words in the lexicon as linked in a large network where the links between items vary in strength. See Figure 7.1, a highly impressionistic example of a network for the word PLANE.

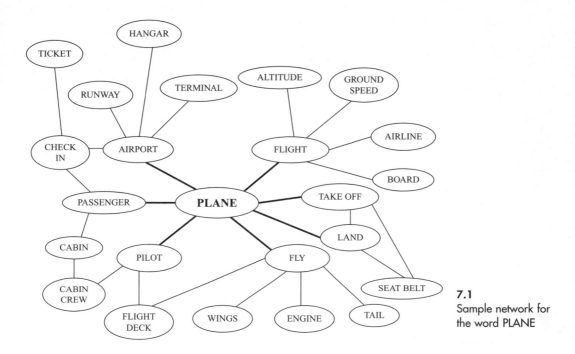

7.1
Sample network for
the word PLANE

EXERCISE

7.10 Look at the semantic network for PLANE, and suggest where the
following items might be attached to it:

> HAND LUGGAGE   NOSE   BOARDING PASS
> STEWARDESS   GATE

How do we establish whether words are closely connected or not?
The traditional approach was to use a WORD ASSOCIATION task. The
experimenter said a word and asked the subject to report the first word
that came into his or her head. Today, researchers often use a task that
produces priming. They might, for example, show subjects a mixture of
words and non-words on a screen and ask them to press a button every
time they see an actual word. The speed with which the subjects press
the button shows how quickly they have identified the word. This
speed increases if, immediately beforehand, they have heard a word that
is associated with the one on the screen.

Word association

EXERCISE

7.11 Here are pairs of words that appear to be associated in the lexicon. The first word (in capitals) primes the second. Can you describe the connection between the first word and the second?

(a)	GREEN *red*	(f)	WING *plane*
(b)	SPARROW *bird*	(g)	CLOCK *watch*
(c)	FISH *chips*	(h)	VEGETABLE *carrot*
(d)	EMPTY *full*	(i)	BUY *sell*
(e)	KNIFE *fork*	(j)	FIND *discover*

It is useful to have technical terms to describe these relationships, which are well established in linguistic theory as well as in psycholinguistics. We have already seen that two words (let us call them A and B) can be described as belonging to the same lexical set. In addition, Word A is:

Synonym • A SYNONYM of Word B if it has the same meaning. Example: *quick/fast*.

Antonym • An ANTONYM of Word B if it has the opposite meaning. Example: *big/small*.

Collocate • A COLLOCATE of Word B if the two words form a collocation. Example: *cup/saucer*.

Superordinate • A SUPERORDINATE of Word B if A is the category that Word B belongs to. Example: *animal/dog*.

Hyponym • A HYPONYM of Word B if A is part of the Word B category. Example: *dog/animal*.

Meronym • A MERONYM of Word B if A is a part of Word B. Example: *handle/door*.

Finally, there is sometimes an odd relationship where Word A entails Word B in reverse. Example: *give/take*. These words are said to be **Converses** CONVERSES.

EXERCISE

7.12 Look again at the examples in Exercise 7.11. Use the correct term for each relationship.

PROJECT

Use *a word association experiment* to investigate which words are connected in the lexicons of your subjects. Devise a list of about 20 words (a mixture of nouns, verbs and adjectives). Make sure that each word has no connection with the one before or after. Check with a corpus (e.g. Leech *et al.*, 2001) to be sure that the words are quite frequent and are similar in frequency. Read aloud the words to around 20–30 subjects, and ask them to say the first word that comes into their heads. Make a recording of each session and afterwards list the words that your subjects have mentioned. See which relationships are most frequent and which are least frequent (using the terminology that you have learnt in this unit.)

An interesting variation might be to compare the answers of subjects in their teens with subjects in their fifties and sixties. Are there any differences in the associations that are made?

In presenting your findings, draw a semantic network for one word, like the one for PLANE in this unit.

8 THE WRITING PROCESS

SPEECH AND WRITING

Let us look at a piece of writing and a piece of speech.

> If you receive a malicious call
> - Remain calm.
> - Try not to encourage the caller with an emotional response.
> - Do not enter into any conversation. Simply put the handset down next to the phone and ignore it for a few minutes before replacing it gently.
> - If the caller doesn't say anything, don't try to get them to speak. Just replace the handset gently if no-one speaks.
> - Don't ever give out any details about yourself or your family unless you are absolutely sure you know and trust the caller.
>
> *The Phone Book* (British Telecom, 2004, abridged)

Husband	sorry
Wife	going to fetch the <u>chil</u>dren this weekend I just been talking to <u>Ra</u>chel
Husband	oh yeah
Wife	and erm thing is she finishes ear::ly on Fri::day and Stuart's got (.) there's a training day at school as well so Stuart's off (.) so:: (.) they could come up earlier (0.5) than y'know than the usual ti::me (0.5) if we can kind of sort out picking them ↑u::p↑ (0.5) what (.) ↑what you doing↑ on Friday

(Langford, 1994: 140–141)

Key

__	stress	::	vowel that is extended
↑ ↑	section of speech that is		in length
	raised in pitch	(.)	brief pause
(0.5)	5-second pause		

EXERCISE

8.1 You will probably have studied the linguistic differences between speech and writing. What examples can you find here? Now consider the psycholinguistic aspects of these differences:

(a) the differences in the *conditions* under which speech and writing are produced. How do these affect the form of the text?

(b) the different *relationship* between writers and readers and between speakers and listeners.

Writing represents a polished end-product. This means that the process of writing has two important components which shape what is produced:

- a PLANNING stage – where words are chosen with some care; **Planning**
- a MONITORING stage – where words are checked and rewritten if necessary. **Monitoring**

Except in odd circumstances (such as exams), those components make use of the greater time that is allowed to the writer as compared to the speaker.

In between the two stages, we need to recognise:

- a TRANSLATING stage – where we choose words and phrases to implement our plan; **Translating**
- an EXECUTING stage – where we actually write or type the words. **Executing**

PLANNING

Planning is more than choosing what to write about. First, a number of RHETORICAL factors need to be considered. **Rhetorical**

EXERCISE

8.2 Compare these four situations. What different factors do the writers have to bear in mind?

(a) Smarm Enterprises wants to write an ad for a new brand of instant coffee to go in the more serious newspapers.

(b) Professor Harry B. Gormenghast wants to write a paper on the maternal instincts of the cuckoo. It is to go in an academic journal.

(c) Sharon Potter wants to write to her local councillor complaining about the way her domestic rubbish is collected.

(d) Zappy Earblaster wants to write a promo. leaflet for his disco event, which is mainly attended by overseas students.

Second, we need to consider how to organise our material. One way of finding out how writers plan is to ask them to talk aloud while they are doing the planning.

EXERCISE

8.3 Compare the comments of these two writers as they plan a story entitled 'A kid who lost things' One is an adult and one is a child; can you guess which is which?

> Do I want an adult [character] to intervene? Or do I want this to be realistic? Or fairy tale-ish? . . . Ah, let me see . . . I know. He makes this model of a ship and on this ship he makes a little model of himself, and he loses it! And this little model of himself happens to end up in his pocket. Oh, why not? I can do anything with this story! Okay, so he just doesn't have any friends and he's still doing things, and he doesn't know where he's put his ship and this little model of himself. But – magic! The little model starts to talk to him and helps him to find things!

> I could put him going to school and he probably loses a shoe. And then he's trying to find it and somebody else finds it. And he goes home and tells his mother and his mother . . . and then the person that finds it gives it back and . . . then the next day, . . . the boy says thank you to the person that found it. Then the next day he goes to school, he loses something else. And the teacher asks him what he lost . . .

> (Scardamalia and Bereiter, 1987: 157–158)

Scardamalia and Bereiter make a distinction between KNOWLEDGE TELLING where a writer simply describes facts one after another as they come to mind; and KNOWLEDGE TRANSFORMING where a writer shapes the raw material into a meaningful pattern.

Knowledge telling

Knowledge transforming

EXERCISE

8.4 What kind of writing do you think you employ (a) when writing an essay? (b) when writing an answer in an exam? Why the difference?

'TRANSLATING'

The ideas that have been produced at the planning stage are then given linguistic shape. This might not take the form of complete sentences in the writer's mind, but might just involve prompts or key words. The writer sometimes makes notes on paper, but often simply stores the target language in a WRITING BUFFER in his or her memory. These mental notes seem to be stored in phonological form: many writers report the impression of having a 'voice in their heads'.

Writing buffer

EXERCISE

8.5 Remember that while these words and phrases are stored in the writer's mind, he/she is also physically putting words down on the page. Why might it be an advantage to store the mental drafts in phonological form?

EXECUTING: THE SPELLING SYSTEM

The writer then has to relate the stored words or phrases to their written shapes. The English writing system is an ALPHABETIC one. In other words, there is relationship between the sounds of the language and the symbols (letters) that are used. The Western European alphabet has 26 letters (some languages do not use all of them) of which 21 are consonants and 5 are vowels. We will compare certain sound–letter relationships from the English system with some from the system that is used to write Castilian Spanish.

Alphabetic

EXERCISES

8.6 Study Table 8.1. Make notes of the differences, and suggest reasons why the English system is so much more complex.

The English system is sometimes described as opaque and the Spanish one as transparent. Can you suggest why?

Table 8.1 English and Spanish spelling systems compared

English (RP) [24 consonant sounds; 12 vowel sounds; 8 diphthongs]		Spanish (Castilian) [20 consonant sounds; 5 vowel sounds; 5 diphthongs]	
/θ/	TH (*Bath*)	/θ/	Z (*zero*) C (+E/I) (*cinco*)
/ð/	TH (*with*)		No equivalent
/k/	C (*cake*) K (*cake*) -CK (*clock*) Q- (*quite*) CH (*chemist*) CC (*occur*)	/k/	C QU- (*queso*) [K in *kilo*]
/ʧ/	CH (*chin*) -TCH (*watch*) -T- (*question*)	/ʧ/	CH (*chico*)
/f/	F (*fork*) -FF- (*off*) PH- (*phone*) -GH (*enough*)	/f/	F (*teléfono*)
/e/	E (*men*) -EA- (*head*) -A- (*many*)	/e/	E (*gente*)
/iː/	-EE- (*see*) EA (*heat*) -IE- (*piece*) -E (*be*) -EI- (*ceiling*) -EY (*key*) E-E (*scene*) I-E (*police*)	/i/	I (*vino*)
/ɑː/	-A- (*bath*) AU- (*aunt*) AR (*arm*) -AL- (*half*) -EAR (*heart*)	/a/	A (*pan*)
/eɪ/	-AY (*pay*) A-E (*late*) -AI- (*wait*) -EA- (*great*) EI- (*weight*) -EY (*grey*)	/ei/	-EI- (*veinte*) -EY (*rey*)

8.7 Study these English words. How do you think a child or a non-native speaker learns the English spelling system for each of these groups?

(a) YACHT BOUGH
(b) RIGHT SIGHT LIGHT
(c) READ LEAD (vb.) BEAD   HEAD DEAD
(d) HOSPITALITY ANTISEPTIC

Sometimes, writers and readers are able to rely upon GRAPHEME–PHONEME CORRESPONDENCE RULES (rules that link a particular sound to a particular spelling). In English, these are more reliable for consonants than for vowels. Sometimes, a sound is represented not by a single grapheme such as P or F but a digraph such as TH- or EA-.

Grapheme–phoneme correspondence rules

Some words can be acquired by analogy to other words which have apparently irregular but consistent spellings. Some words are unique and have to be learnt as single units.

EXERCISE

8.8 (a) Give examples of other digraphs in English.
   (b) Give other examples of words that can be acquired by analogy.
   (c) Can you think of other words that are unique?

EXECUTING: WRITING THE WORDS

We now consider the relationship between the brain and the fingers. We can learn a lot by looking at the kinds of errors that typists make.

EXERCISE

8.9 Examine these examples of typing errors. What do you think are the causes?

   (a) THE → teh   LANGUAGE → langauge
        FROM THE → fro mthe
   (b) there → THEIR   WRITE → right
        COULD → good
   (c) BY → be   FOR → of   THESE → there
        WHERE → were
   (d) WORRY → wurry   SPREAD → spred
        DISTANCE → distins

MONITORING

The final stage of writing involves monitoring. Monitoring might lead the writer:

- to go back and change their plan;
- to revise the words that are used;
- to correct spelling and typing mistakes.

So it operates at several different levels.

EXERCISE

8.10 Below is an example of an authentic text which has been redrafted. Identify what kinds of change the author made and explain them. Use these broad terms to suggest at what levels the changes were made:

Planning:	the writer changes his emphasis or adds to the content.
Register:	the writer makes the text more formal or more technical.
Stylistic:	the writer presents his ideas in a more polished way.
Organisational:	the writer changes the order of ideas or makes links between them.
Execution:	the writer corrects errors of typing.

> The ability to plan writing is something that children develop ~~during their first years as writers~~ quite slowly. At first, ~~thye~~ they give ~~a lot of~~ considerable attention to forming letters on ~~teh~~ the page, and tend to say words aloud or to mouth them as they are writing them~~, suggesting~~ . This suggests that much of their ~~mental effort is going into~~ working memory is taken up with the process of forming the words and little ~~of their working memory~~ with the process of planning. The slowness with which ~~thye~~ they write must also make it difficult for them to ~~think ahead~~ organise their ideas. ~~However, a~~ After about two years, ~~thye~~ they begin to ~~menth~~ mouth not single words but a whole string of words, suggesting that they are now carrying some kind of sentence plan in their heads, which they need to ~~repeat~~ rehearse so as not to ~~loose~~ lose it.

PROJECT

Study the execution errors of five of your fellow students. First, ask them to do a brief typing test, copying a page from a book. Time them and compare their speeds.

When they write their next essay, ask them not to correct any typing errors until they have finished their first draft. Get them to print out the draft and analyse the errors. Look especially for phonologically based errors and errors that suggest that the subject has developed an automatic key stroke sequence which is incorrect. Check these sequences to see if they can be accounted for in terms of the position of the letters on the keyboard. Compare the percentages of different types of error among your five subjects. Then check with your figures on typing speed and decide whether or not that is a factor.

9 THE SPEAKING PROCESS

INFORMATION PROCESSING

The way in which psycholinguists view the four language skills (speaking, listening, reading and writing) has been heavily influenced by what is known as the INFORMATION PROCESSING approach.

Information processing

Here is a simple example of information processing.

1 A timer switch turns off the bottom light of a set of three and turns on the top light.
2 The light shines out through red glass.
3 A driver sees that the red light is brighter.
4 The driver interprets: RED = stop.
5 The driver puts on the brakes.

We could show this as a flow-chart (which is how writers display many types of psychological process). The important points are that:

(a) there is a process which passes through several stages;
(b) at each successive stage, the form of the information changes.

Something similar is said to occur with the raw material of language. It is taken through several stages, at each of which it is reshaped. The reshaping continues until (in listening and reading) a rich interpretation is derived or (in speaking and writing) a comprehensible string of words is constructed.

ASSEMBLING SPEECH

Articulation

So we envisage a speaker as building a sentence step by step, each stage bringing them closer to the moment of ARTICULATION when the sentence is actually uttered.

Assume that a policewoman is watching CCTV footage of a bank robbery. She sees a thief put some money into a bag. She wants to describe what she sees. The sentence she decides to produce is:

He is putting the money into a bag.

EXERCISE

9.1 What decisions has the policewoman made about the words to use in her utterance?

(a) First think about her choice of the word PUT. What is the effect of choosing PUT on the pattern of the sentence? Compare the impossible sentences

*He is putting. *He is putting the money.

[* indicates that a sentence is unacceptable]

What stops her from planning sentences like these?

(b) What stops her from producing a sentence like:

*He the money is putting a bag into?

(c) Now think about how she finds the words she needs: MONEY and BAG.

(d) Suggest why she chooses the form *is putting* (rather than *put* or *was putting*).

(e) Suggest why she decides to use the words *he*, *the* and *a*.

We can conclude that, in designing a sentence, a speaker has to consider:

- syntax (the grammatical structure of the sentence), which may be determined by the main verb;
- rules about WORD ORDER;   **Word order**
- what words from the lexicon are needed;
- the FORM OF THE VERB;   **Form of the verb**
- inflections;
- what has already been mentioned (what is 'GIVEN') and what has   **Given**
  not (what is 'NEW').   **New**

We must remember that, at this stage, the sentence is abstract. It is a plan, with links to the grammar and vocabulary that are stored in the speaker's mind. It is not yet in the form of actual words. From the plan, the speaker has to construct the final form of the sentence, which might be

He's putting the MONey into a BAG.

Or more accurately (as there aren't regular gaps between words in speech):

He'sputtingtheMONeyintoaBAG.

We could show this in phoneme notation as:

/hiːz|pʊtɪŋðə|mʌnɪɪntʊə|bæg/

EXERCISE

9.2 So the speaker has now retrieved the forms of the words from her lexicon and has organised them in the order laid down in the plan. But what else has she done?

(a) Consider the first word *he's*.
(b) Consider why *MONey* and *BAG* are given heavy stress.
(c) Consider the difference between how we show the words in written form and how they are actually said. Look especially at the way in which *the* and *a* are pronounced.

Phonological plan   The speaker has now created a PHONOLOGICAL PLAN, which anticipates the spoken form of the sentence. But there is a small problem here. It is not at all easy to say some of the words together.

EXERCISE

9.3 Try saying these words quite fast:

MONeyinto /|mʌnɪɪntʊ/   intoa /ɪntʊə/

Did you change them in any way?

Reduce   Speakers often simplify (or REDUCE) what they say if it involves a complicated movement between one position of the tongue and another. **Phonetic plan** So, before she utters the sentence, our speaker forms a PHONETIC PLAN – a plan not of the 'perfect' form of the sentence but of how she will actually say it.

You might think that this reduction process makes life difficult for the listener. Well, sometimes it does. But it is important to realise that reduction is quite systematic. There are certain quite common ways in which a listener can expect a speaker to reduce the words they utter.

EXERCISE

9.4 Examine these examples of reduced speech. How does the speaker change their phonological plan? Which of the examples are similar?

(a) next spring → neck spring
(b) ten pounds → tem pounds
(c) went out → wen tout
(d) do you know what I mean? → narp mean?
(e) made it → may dit
(f) half past → huppast
(g) asked a question → arst a question
(h) that girl → thak girl

What happens next? Well, the plan is turned into a set of instructions to about 100 tiny muscles that control the ARTICULATORS, the organs that we use to produce speech. The instructions coordinate the articulators to produce the sounds of the sentence.

Articulators

EXERCISE

9.5 Which parts of the mouth and breathing system do you think these muscles are connected to?

We have studied the way in which a speaker ASSEMBLES the material of a sentence. We have identified several stages:

Assembles

- a CONCEPTUAL stage where the speaker first has an idea that she wants to express;

Conceptual

- a PLANNING stage, where a grammatical pattern is laid down and links to the lexicon are set up;

Planning

- a PHONOLOGICAL stage where the spoken form of the sentence is anticipated;

Phonological

Phonetic • a PHONETIC stage where the spoken form might be simplified to make speaking easier;

Articulatory • an ARTICULATORY stage when the tongue, lips and jaw are making the sentence.

EXERCISE

9.6 Think of the example of the policewoman. Recall what she does at each of the stages that have been identified.

We have seen how an utterance is planned. But what happens to the plan while we are actually speaking? Let us say that the policewoman is producing the word *putting*. She has only just begun her utterance but she needs to be clear about how she is going to finish it.

Speech buffer The answer usually given is that she holds her plan for the complete utterance in a SPEECH BUFFER in her mind, like the buffer in a computer which stores information for the printer. The plan then feeds through gradually to the articulators.

So how much do we put into this buffer at a time? We have assumed so far that it is a sentence; but is that always the case? And when do we plan the next chunk of speech: while we are actually talking or afterwards?

EXERCISE

9.7 Study this piece of spoken English. At what points do you think the speaker is planning new units of speech? What appears to be the size of these units?

> I'm just <u>tea</u>ching:: (.) two of my daughters to dri:ve (.) ↑one's↑ already got a provisional licence ↑cos she's seventeen:::↑ (.)↑the other's↑ <u>six</u>teen so she can't get a provisional licence until her <u>birth</u>day (.) h so:: (.) with <u>her</u> the <u>young</u>est <u>Sarah</u> (.) we have to go to a big <u>car</u> park at the supermarket: (.) we just <u>drive</u> round <u>there</u> (.) but it's ↑quite↑ useful ↑↑I mean:↑ (.) she can get to know the <u>ba</u>:sics there
>
> (Langford, 1994: 102–103)

Key

__	stress	::	vowel or consonant that
↑ ↑	section of speech that is		is extended in length
	raised in pitch	(.)	brief pause

We need to make a distinction between pauses that are used for planning and pauses that mark hesitation.

EXERCISE

9.8 Compare these two speakers, one an interviewer and one a scientist. Which is the more hesitant? Why do you think so? Identify the differents ways in which these speakers hesitate. Which pauses do you think are hesitation pauses and which are planning pauses? What do you notice about the position of the hesitation pauses? Now suggest why you think hesitation pauses might occur?

Interviewer	the other area I should say in this book th- that there's a great deal of is erm interest in + popular science and erm my next guest is + not a POPular scientist a PROper scientist
Scientist	a proper scientist + certainly yes
Interviewer	a proper scientist [ ] absolutely + and indeed deals with something that I suppose [ ] we would find properly mysterious erm worthy of erm investigation and elucidation + which is SOUND in the universe + most of us would look up from this planet erm and assume that out there + everything is silent but not so
Scientist	yes it's it's a very common misconception that there's there's no sound in space but that's not entirely true + there's no sound in a vacuum because sound unlike light travels by the:: compression of a medium + and there are plenty of places out there in the universe that are rich in gas + and [ ] it can form an atmosphere of some kind + even if it's a very thin dilute atmosphere + and sound waves can travel through this.

(BBC Radio 4, *Start the Week*, 9 February 2004)

Key

+	pause	::	extended vowel length
CAPS	heavy emphatic stress	[ ]	part of transcript omitted

SELF-MONITORING

Just as in writing, speakers monitor the language they have produced to see if it suits their purposes.

EXERCISE

9.9 Here are six examples of speakers correcting themselves as a result of self-monitoring (sources: Levelt, 1989; Underwood, 1975; Cutler, 1980; Boomer and Laver, 1968).

- Describe the error in each case.
- At what point do speakers usually seem to correct themselves?
- Compare (a) and (b). Can you identify two different stages of the speaking process when speakers monitor their utterances?

(a) Why it is – is it – that nobody makes a decent toilet seat?
(b) Well, I don't think you could erm – I don't think there's any – er depends upon what time of day.
(c) Hey, why didn't you show up last week? . . . Either of you two.
(d) Well, let me write it back – er down – so that . . .
(e) You're in a real adVANtag – advanTAGeous position.
(f) Didn't bother me in the sleast – er slightest.

PROJECT

Record a formal piece of speech (for example, an unscripted lecture or an interview on the radio). Then record an informal piece of speech (for example, somebody telling a story to friends). Transcribe a section of about 90 seconds from each one. Mark the pauses clearly and time them. Underline the words that carry heavy stress. Then time each sentence. Count how many syllables it contains and work out a speaking rate for the sentence in syllables per second.

Compare the two pieces of discourse in terms of:

- The number of planning pauses; how long they are.
- The number of hesitation pauses; how long they are; where they occur.
- How regularly a heavily stressed word occurs.
- How much reduction takes place.
- How fast each speaker is speaking (in syllables per second). Check whether they speak faster at the beginning, middle or end of the piece you have recorded.

Write up your findings.

LANGUAGE PROCESSING

10

'Processing' is a general term for the mental operations that are involved in handling language. But it is sometimes used to refer specifically to the operations that readers and listeners use when constructing meanings from letters on the page or sounds in the ear. In the next three sections, we focus especially on these receptive skills.

The approach we adopted in Unit 9 viewed the speaker as building an utterance in several stages: focusing first on the idea, then the grammar, then the words, then the sounds and so on. These stages are often referred to as LEVELS OF REPRESENTATION. The same kind of staged model is used when psycholinguists come to analyse reading and listening.

Levels of representation

BOTTOM-UP PROCESSING

One way of approaching listening is to assume that a listener operates like a speaker in reverse. They can be seen as building small units (i.e. the sounds of language) into larger and larger ones. This kind of operation is referred to as BOTTOM-UP PROCESSING.

Bottom-up processing

EXERCISE

10.1 Here are some levels of representation that may be involved in bottom-up processing by a listener.

Arrange them in order, with the smallest unit first and largest last.

(a) syntactic pattern   (d) utterance meaning
(b) phoneme   (e) syllable
(c) word

Now consider the following situation. At a party, a man offers a cigarette to a woman. She responds with a string of sounds which we can represent like this in phonemic script: /gɪvn¦ʌpsməʊkɪŋ/. We can transcribe them as: givenUPsmoking.

Here is how the man might analyse the string of sounds:

1   *Syllable level.* The man divides the chunk of speech into syllables:

    /gɪv + nʌp + sməʊ + kɪŋ/

2   *Word forms.* The man works out what words are contained in the chunk:

    /gɪvn + ʌp + sməʊkɪŋ/

3   *Word meanings.* The man has to access the meanings of the words:

    GIVE UP = stop   SMOKE = consume burning tobacco

4   *Syntactic level.* The man has to recognise an underlying grammatical pattern:

    [I have] given up smoking.

5   The man has to understand the literal meaning of the whole utterance:

    I have stopped consuming burning tobacco.

(Note that this is a greatly simplified account. Not everybody would agree that all the levels we have discussed are necessary.)

EXERCISE

10.2 So the man has learnt that the woman has stopped consuming tobacco. Is this literal meaning enough? Is there one last step that he has to take if he is to understand what she meant?

EXERCISE

10.3 Here is another string of sounds. You have an appointment at 9.15. A friend says to you [sɑːfpɑːsnaɪn] – SARFPASSNINE. Describe the stages that you take this message through.

TOP-DOWN PROCESSING: WORD KNOWLEDGE

The process we have examined so far focuses on what is actually there in the speech signal. It involves building small units into larger ones. But the examples given are a simplification. Here is a reading task that will show why.

EXERCISE

10.4 Read aloud the words in Figure 10.1. Then spell them, saying the names of the letters in them.

10.1
Top-down processing (from Rumelhardt and McClelland, 1986: 8)

Now compare the D in RED with the B in DEBT. Any comments? Look at other letters that had blots on them. Why do you think you read them as you did?

Top-down   Information does not just flow in a bottom-up direction from small units to larger ones. It can also proceed in a TOP-DOWN one from larger units to smaller. In the task you just did, your knowledge of the words influenced the way you interpreted the letters.

TOP-DOWN PROCESSING: CONTEXT

The clearest examples of top-down processing occur when a listener or reader uses knowledge that is not in the actual text but comes from outside it. For example, a reader understands a text on stamp collecting or trout fishing better if he/she has some previous knowledge of the topic. So we need to make a distinction between:

Perceptual   •   PERCEPTUAL INFORMATION that is actually in the text and that
information   the listener/reader has to decode;

Conceptual   •   CONCEPTUAL INFORMATION that the listener/reader brings to the
information   text from outside knowledge.

EXERCISE

10.5 Here are various examples of situations where a listener has to use conceptual information to fully understand what is being said. In each case, describe the type of information that is used. What knowledge is the speaker taking for granted in the listener?

  (a) The speaker mentions *that woman who lives next door to me.*
  (b) The speaker mentions *phonemes.*
  (c) The speaker mentions *the village shop.*
  (d) The speaker mentions *what you just said about the new by-pass.*
  (e) The speaker mentions *the African elephant.*
  (f) The speaker says *I must warn you that anything you say may be taken down . . .*
  (g) The speaker reads the Minutes of the last meeting, introduces Item 1 of this meeting, then invites other committee members to give their views.

PARALLEL PROCESSING

There is another way in which the bottom-up sequence illustrated in the GIVEN UP SMOKING example in Exercise 10.1 is a simplification. It assumes that the listener waits until the end of an utterance before working out what it means. However, there is evidence that listeners process what they hear as the speaker is saying it. This means that, at any given time, different bits of what the speaker says are probably being processed at different stages. Let us say that, at a given point, the listener is matching the last part of the utterance /smǝʊkiŋ/ with a word in his lexicon. At the same time, he might be working out the meaning of the first part GIVEN UP.

Reading provides a clearer example of this kind of PARALLEL processing.

Parallel

EXERCISES

10.6 Here are some mistyped words. What words do you think the typist intended?

> REVENCE   REVENOE   LOMELY   LOYELY

10.7 Imagine you see the following words in a rough draft of a letter. What words do you think the writer intended? How did you arrive at this guess? Did you find one group easier than the others? Was one harder?

   (a)   STRANCE   COMEORT   APRIVE
   (b)   GRADEN   DOMETSIC   RUBGLARY
   (c)   DIFFICUST   GECOVERY   HOLINAY
   (d)   SHEORY   THEERFUL   SHOLKING   PUNIST

One theory holds that a reader processes a written word at four different levels:

- letter FEATURES (the curves, straight lines and obliques that make up letters);
- letters;
- letter order;
- whole words.

Features

Readers also seem to pay heed to common letter groups such as TH-, STR-, SH-, -NGE etc. You probably used all of these considerations in trying to decode the words in the exercise. The important point to note is that the processing takes place at these four or five different levels *at the same time* – IN PARALLEL. So, at the same time as you were looking

In parallel

at the word as a whole, you were also checking the order of the letters. At the same time as you were noticing letter features, you were also distinguishing whole letters.

TOP-DOWN VS BOTTOM-UP

We now come to perhaps the most controversial issue in language processing. We have seen that listeners and readers make use of their top-down knowledge of the world as well as bottom-up evidence based on what is in the text. But how do the two mix? Do we need to finish bottom-up processing before we bring in outside ideas? Or do outside ideas influence bottom-up processing from the start?

EXERCISE

10.8 The fact is that experts simply don't agree on the relationship between the two types of processing. There are several possible views. Study the four scenarios below. Each one represents a theory of how top-down knowledge influences bottom-up processing. Distinguish them in terms of when top-down evidence is used by the listener.

(a) A listener hears a weather forecaster say *Heavy cloud is coming in from the Atlantic bringing* . . .. She does not need to listen any further.

(b) A listener hears somebody say: *Put it in the right box.* He notices that all the boxes are on the left-hand side of the table.

(c) A listener hears a friend say: *I found that dreadful exam very* . . . On hearing the next syllable DIFF- she opens up a cohort of words (DIFFERENT, DIFFICULT, DIFFIDENT) before taking the context into account.

(d) The listener hears a news reader say: *Carrots and potatoes are quite cheap in the shops but other vegables are in short supply.* He does not notice that VEGETABLES has been mispronounced.

Broadly, there are two main views about top-down and bottom-up information.

1   We have to keep the two apart. So, when we are processing the sounds somebody is saying, we do not get confused by also having to consider what the context tells us. Of course, that does not

prevent us from using contextual information afterwards. See scenario (b) in Exercise 10.8.

2   When we are working out meaning, we need to have all possible pieces of information available (both bottom-up and top-down). That way we can make a fully informed decision. This interactive view is compatible with scenarios (a) (using world knowledge) and (d) (using vocabulary knowledge).

PROJECT

Investigate situations where what we hear is in conflict with the contextual cues that are available. Find out if we seem to rely on bottom-up or top-down information.

Design sentences with words in them that differ by one or two phonemes. Ensure that one of the two choices of word is strongly supported by the context. Here are some examples, but you may want to devise more of your own. You may also need to adjust the phoneme contrasts to your local variety of English:

I'm going to sail my ship./I'm going to sell my ship.
She was injured by the accident./She was hindered by the accident.
In this church I married my husband./In this church I buried my husband.
On the plane, we had a terrible flight./On the plane, we had a terrible fright.
I pay a lot of tax on what I earn./I pay a lot of tax on what I own.
Astronomers keep wondering about the planet./Astronomers keep wandering about the planet.
He washed his clothes in the machine./He watched his clothes in the machine.
My employer encourages me to work from home./My employer encourages me to walk from home.
We lived in the jungle with no thought of home./We lived in the jungle with no sort of home.
He showed us a view of the mountains./He showed us a few of the mountains.

Choose 50 per cent of the predictable versions and 50 per cent of the unpredictable ones. Mix the sentences randomly and record them on to a cassette with pauses of about six seconds between each one. Then make a second recording with all the remaining sentences on it, again mixed up randomly and with pauses between them.

Play the first recording to at least 10 subjects and ask them to repeat exactly what they heard. Make notes of what each one says or (better still) record them. Repeat, using the second recording, with the same number of different subjects. Study the 'unlikely' sentences, and compare what the subjects said. See to what extent they relied on phonological evidence and to what extent on contextual evidence. Draw conclusions about how strong bottom-up information is as against top-down. Consider the implications for, e.g., radio broadcasting.

THE READING PROCESS

The following views of what makes a skilled reader have greatly influenced the teaching of reading.

- *Theory A.* Good readers recognise words by their shapes. Once we have learnt to read, we do not need to pay attention to the individual letters in a word. Similarly, when we come to read silently, the way a word is pronounced is no longer relevant.
- *Theory B.* Good readers use long sweeps of their eyes, taking in many words. That is how they can read faster than less skilled readers.
- *Theory C.* Good readers make use of context so that they do not need to read every word in a text. They save themselves processing effort by anticipating words.

EXERCISE

11.1 Consider each of the theories above and give your own opinions. Draw upon your own experience as a reader.

WORD RECOGNITION

Unit 8 on writing looked at the difficulties that an OPAQUE alphabet can cause a writer. We now consider the issue from the point of view of someone who needs to *recognise* written words. English has an opaque system with unique words like YACHT. So does this mean that readers only pay heed to whole words when they are reading? The idea led to the WHOLE WORD approach to teaching reading, where children were

Opaque

Whole word

Phonics taught to recognise complete words rather than (as in the PHONICS approach) being shown what sound each letter represents.

EXERCISE

11.2 Read aloud the following verse:

> He took his vorpal sword in hand;
> Long time the manxome foe he sought –
> So rested he by the Tumtum tree,
> And stood awhile in thought.
> And, as in uffish thought he stood,
> The Jabberwock, with eyes of flame,
> Came whiffling through the tulgy wood,
> And burbled as it came!

Now try to explain how you were able to read aloud *vorpal*, *manxome*, *Tumtum*, *uffish*, *Jabberwock*, *whiffling* and *tulgy*, words which you had probably never seen before.

As you saw in Unit 5, one theory of reading suggests that, when we read, we use two different routes:

Lexical route • A LEXICAL ROUTE, where we recognise words as a whole.

Sub-lexical route • A SUB-LEXICAL ROUTE where we use sound–spelling rules to work out, letter by letter, how to pronounce words. The lexical route is faster; but we need the sub-lexical route in order to work out how to say unfamiliar words including:

Proper nouns • PROPER NOUNS (names of people and places);
  • new technical terms;
  • words we know in speech but have never seen written.

EXERCISE

11.3 Read aloud the following non-words. If possible, transcribe them using phonemic notation. Check your answers with others. On some words you are likely to agree; on others you may disagree.

GEAD   NEAN   SOAT   PIVE   FOWN   HEAF   WIRT

Ask yourself how you decided on how to pronounce these words.

We do not just use sound–spelling rules in decoding English words; we also use ANALOGY with words that are spelt in similar ways. You can see this in the way you almost certainly disagreed on how to pronounce some of the non-words above and agreed on others. For example, you probably came up with two possible pronunciations of GEAD:

Analogy

(a) GEAD = /giːd/ by analogy with neighbours like BEAD, LEAD (vb.), READ (pres.)
(b) GEAD = /ged/ by analogy with neighbours like DEAD, LEAD (n.), HEAD

EXERCISES

11.4 Find as many 'neighbours' as you can for the other non-words. Relate them to your preferred pronunciations.

11.5 At the beginning of this unit, two methods of teaching reading were mentioned: the whole word method and the phonics method. Comment on them in the light of the tasks you have just done.

The important point to note from this section is that the links between letters and sounds are not just something that we use when we are learning to read. They are something that continues to assist our reading as adults.

EYE MOVEMENTS

We now look at what happens physically when we read. Thanks to sophisticated tracking equipment, researchers can find out exactly how a reader's eye moves across a page. The eye moves in rapid sweeps (known as SACCADES) from one fixation point to another. It rests at a FIXATION point for a varying amount of time, depending on the length and frequency of the word it is viewing. A fixation lasts on average for about 250 milliseconds (i.e. a quarter of a second). The eye focuses on about 7 characters in the text at the fixation point; but it also takes in up to 9 more on either side.

Saccades
Fixation

Figure 11.1 shows the pattern of eye movements of a competent adult reader. The small circles above the text show where the fixation points

286 221   246   277   256   233 216   188
 o   o   o   o   o   o   o   o

Roadside joggers endure sweat, pain and angry drivers in the name of

301   177 196   175   244   302 112 177   266 188   199
       o   o   ←
 o   o   o   o   o o   o   o   o

fitness. A healthy body may seem reward enough for most people. However,

216   212   179 109 266   245   188   205
 o   ←
           o   o   o   o   o   o   o

for all those who question the payoff, some recent research on physical

201 66   201 188   203   220   217   288
 o   ←
      o   o   o   o   o   o   o

activity and creativity has provided some surprisingly good news.

11.1
Eye movement data
(adapted from
Rayner and
Pollatsek,
1989: 116)

occurred, and the numbers above them show how long (in milliseconds) each fixation lasted. Leftwards arrows show where, occasionally, the eye **Regressed** of the reader REGRESSED.

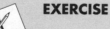

EXERCISE

11.6 (a) Roughly how many characters does a typical saccade cover?
   (b) What evidence is there that an experienced reader makes long saccades and takes in several words at a time?
   (c) What type of word is most frequently skipped? Can you suggest why?
   (d) As noted above, the reader's eyes also take in information that is just outside the fixation area. An English reader tends to pay more heed to letters and spaces to the right of the fixation. How might this help the reading process?
   (e) Which words had the longest fixations? Which were fixated twice? Can you suggest why?
   (f) The reader's eye regresses in three places. Can you suggest why?

Reading this text, a competent reader makes short saccades (of about 7–9 characters), fixates the text for an average of about 250 msec and makes few regressions (only about 10 per cent of fixations). The regressions are usually to check that the context has been understood. But we must be careful not to over-generalise.

EXERCISES

11.7 Read Text A below. Time yourself.

> Education seems beset by problems associated with language, both in the words used to describe common purposes and activities, and in imports from elsewhere. We speak of key skills, autonomy, transitions, assuming that their definitions are accepted. . . .
>
> Teaching programmes are no longer implemented but 'rolled out', like a new car or aircraft produced by experts, emerging from behind closed doors. Likewise programmes of study are no longer taught – a process implying interaction between students and teachers – they are 'delivered'. Mail is delivered, babies are delivered and explosives are delivered by missile systems, but teaching programmes? While having their programmes delivered, students are 'tracked'. Their performances are scrutinised and judged to see how on or off track they are. If a track is like a rail, then such terminology implies little room for diversity, discovery or insights on the student's part.
>
> (Patrick Smith, *Times Higher Education Supplement*, 5 Dec., 2003)

Try to recall the reading process. Were your fixations long or short? To what extent were you aware of regressing?

11.8 Now read Text B below. Again, time yourself.

> I think that I can date my interest in the case from that first mention of the ABC railway guide. Up till then, I had not been able to raise much enthusiasm. The sordid murder of an old woman in a back street shop was so like the usual type of crime reported in the newspapers that it failed to strike a significant note. In my own mind I had put down the anonymous letter with its mention of the 21st as a mere coincidence. Mrs Archer, I felt reasonably sure, had been the victim of her drunken

brute of a husband. But now the mention of the railway guide (so familiarly known by its abbreviation of ABC, listing as it did all the railway stations in their alphabetical order) sent a quiver of excitement through me. Surely – surely this could not be a second coincidence? The sordid crime took on a new aspect. Who was the mysterious individual who had killed Mrs Archer and left an ABC railway guide behind him?

(Agatha Christie, *The ABC Murders*, 1936)

Was the reading process at all different? Were your fixations longer or shorter than with Text A? Did you regress more or less? Which of the two texts do you think was the longer?

The fact is that a good reader is *flexible*, adapting their reading style (including fixation duration, length of saccade and number of regressions) to the kind of text that is being read.

EXERCISE

11.9 Table 11.1 shows the average fixation duration, saccade length, percentage of regression and speed for four types of text.

(a) a Physics text;
(b) a piece of English literature;
(c) a piece of light fiction;
(d) a newspaper article.

Can you decide which is which?

Table 11.1 Variations in reading style

TEXT	Fixation duration (msec)	Saccade length (no. of characters)	Regression (% of saccades)	Speed (words per min.)
1	202	9.2	3	365
2	209	8.3	6	321
3	220	7.9	10	305
4	261	6.9	17	238

Source: derived from Raynor and Pollatsek, 1989: 118

UNSKILLED READING

If both good readers and poor readers fixate almost every word, then what makes a poor reader so much slower? We will try to find out by asking you to perform a task that turns you into a poor reader.

EXERCISE

11.10 Read Text C. Immediately after you have read it, make notes of what you did in order to work out its meaning.

> Upon a day bifel, that he for his desport is went in-to the feeldes him to pleye. His wyf and eek his doghter hath he left inwith his hous, of which the dores weren fast y-shette. Three of his olde foos han it espyed, and setten laddres to the walles of his hous, and by the windowes been entred, and betten his wyf, and wounded his doghter with fyve mortal woundes in fyve sondry places; this is to seyn, in hir feet, in hir handes, in hir eres, in hir nose, and in hir mouth; and leften hir for deed, and wenten away. Whan Melibeus retourned was in-to his hous and saugh al this meschief, he, lyk a mad man, rendinge his clothes, gan to wepe and crye.
>
> (Chaucer, *Tale of Melibeus*)

A good reader does not normally have problems in recognising words. But weak readers have problems of decoding, like those you experienced with this piece of Middle English. They respond by:

* making approximate matches to word forms that they know;
* skipping many words where they fail to make a match;
* using syntax to work out what a word is likely to be;
* using context to work out what a word is likely to be.

The important point to note here is that, like you reading Text C, poor readers are heavily dependent upon context to give them clues.

EXERCISE

11.11 Weak readers make many more regressions than skilled readers. Can you suggest why? Good readers also regress, though less frequently. They do so for reasons that are different from those of weak readers. Can you suggest what these reasons might be?

AUTOMATICITY

For a good reader, decoding is not just rapid; it is also automatic. Let us consider what is meant by this.

EXERCISE

11.12 Look at the graphics on p. 101. Your task is not to report what the words say but to report, as quickly as possible, *what the shapes are that surround the words.*

You probably found that the words within the boxes interfered with your ability to say what the shapes were. This is because your processing of the words (associating their forms with their meanings) is so automatic that you have great difficulty in turning it off. Recall, if you can, the effort involved in your first reading experiences as a child and (if you learnt with phonics) the heavy demands upon your attention made by the many different sound–spelling rules. What happened is that, over time and by dint of practice, processes that were once deliberate and conscious

Automatised became AUTOMATISED.

But why is it beneficial to employ processes that are automatic? The

Working memory reason is that WORKING MEMORY (the part of memory that we use for processing incoming information) is limited in how much it can hold. An automatic process makes very few demands upon working memory. This means that a reader who decodes automatically has a great deal of memory capacity spare for thinking about the meaning of the text as a whole. But a reader who has to allocate a lot of attention to decoding words does not. See Figure 11.2, where the black sections represent the demands of decoding and the white, the attention that is left free for constructing overall meaning.

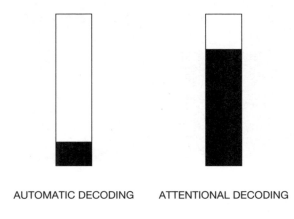

AUTOMATIC DECODING   ATTENTIONAL DECODING

11.2
Demands of
decoding and
memory capacity
left free

So, in current reading theory, automatic decoding is seen as the key to skilled reading.

ANOTHER VIEW OF SKILLED READING

Kenneth Goodman (1967) took a different view, suggesting that reading is a 'guessing game'. He argued that the skilled reader is somebody who uses context in order to guess what is coming next. As a result, they do not need to decode every single word in the text, as they can anticipate many of them. This view has influenced some teachers of reading, who say that children should be encouraged to extract overall meaning from a text rather than developing decoding skills.

EXERCISE

11.13 Put the 'prediction' claim to the test. Text D is a short extract from a newspaper article (*Observer*, 5 July 1987), reproduced in vertical columns instead of horizontal lines. Put a sheet of paper over the top line. Move it downwards, each time trying to predict what the next word will be. Put a tick against any words that you were able to predict. When you have read the piece, classify the words as content words or function words. What do you find?

Text D

In	tiny	than
the	objects	the
past,	compared	Earth.
the	with	Second,
search	stars:	planets
for	for	do
other	instance,	not
worlds	the	shine,
has	sun,	but
been	a	only
hampered	typical	reflect
by	star,	light
two	is	dimly
factors.	300,000	from
First,	times	stars.
Planets	more	
are	massive	

Even if good readers cannot predict the exact words, it could still be argued that they predict the *ideas* that are coming next, thus reducing the need to decode what is on the page. So let us evaluate Goodman's theory further.

EXERCISE

11.14 We have seen that readers need a lot of spare working memory for building overall meaning and for interpreting the text. What would happen if we replaced decoding with anticipation? Would more memory be available to the reader or less?

To summarise current theory believes that skilled reading relies upon *accurate* and *automatic* decoding (contrast your efforts with Text C). Skilled readers do indeed make use of context – but they use it to enrich their understanding of the text. It is weak readers who use context so as not to have to decode words. They do it because their decoding is so slow and effortful.

PROJECT

Use a method known as MISCUE ANALYSIS. Choose a text of **Miscue analysis** medium difficulty, about a page long. Ask around 20 subjects to read the text aloud quite quickly and record them reading. Time each reader and work out their speed in words per second. Then go through the recordings, listening for any errors made by the subjects (including those where the subject self-corrects afterwards). Classify the errors as:

- Words that have been omitted.
- Substituted words that are not like the target word in form but:
  fit the meaning of the context and/or
  fit the grammar of the context.

- Substituted words that do not fit grammar or meaning but are similar in form to the target word.
- Extra words that have been inserted.

Work out the percentages of each as a total of the errors.

Miscue analysis was used extensively by Goodman to argue that readers focused more on the context than on the actual form of words. Does your result support this finding or not? Now go on to look at reading speed. Is there any relationship between the speed at which a subject reads and the number and type of error?

We have to be cautious with miscue analysis as an indicator of how people read. To see why this is, get five more subjects to read the same text silently. Time them and compare their speeds with those of the readers who read aloud.

12 THE LISTENING PROCESS

Automatic   Listening is a highly AUTOMATIC process – so automatic that we tend
to take it for granted. But it is by no means easy to explain how listeners
Decoding   achieve what they do. Let us first consider DECODING: how it is that
the listener is able to recognise the sounds and words that occur in the
speech signal.

EXERCISES

12.1 Here is a piece of speech from a comic book entitled *Fraffly Well
Spoken*. The writer is parodying the speakers' upper-class British
accents; but the extract illustrates many other problems beside
accent that face listeners. Read it aloud two or three times and
try to work out what the speakers are saying. Hint: it is about
cigars.

Margaret	Hermny skoss dew smirkner deh?
Henry	Con seck sickly. Bot torth rare, preps. Preps thrair.
Margaret	Henrair, one door swish shoed tretter smirk less. Sotch bixer gozz too. Shorred kompy good for one. Sholly wonken remembah what Cholz said a botcher hot.
Henry	Isty Ah. Ear stirrof koss.
Margaret	Henrair, prommer smair you'll tretter cottem donter tour deh.

(A. Lauder, 1968: 34)

12.2 Suggest the features of the conversation in Exercise 12.1 which
made it difficult to understand.

There are some similarities between the ways in which readers and listeners build higher-level meaning. But the processes of *decoding* are very different – as one would expect, given that the medium is so different.

We will compare how readers and listeners decode a text. First, examine this piece of reading.

> Car theft is on the increase in this area. Please ensure that, when leaving your vehicle, you lock it.

EXERCISE

12.3 What clues are there in a written text like this which help the reader:

    (a)   to distinguish the different letters (e.g. *t, h, f*);
    (b)   to work out where words begin and end;
    (c)   to work out where a phrase ends;
    (d)   to work out where a clause ends;
    (e)   to work out where a sentence ends;
    (f)   to identify which are the important words in the text?

Now look at the kind of utterance that a listener might have to process:

thəneckstrainfə**LON**dən + isthəsebm**FOR**tyfrəmpla'form **EIGHT** +

ə = weak sound at the beginning of *about*

+ = pause

bold type = stressed syllable

bold type and CAPS = heavy stress

EXERCISES

12.4 What are the main differences between the spoken signal and the written one?

12.5 What clues are there in a spoken utterance which help the listener to decide:

(a) where syllables begin and end;
(b) where words begin and end;
(c) where phrases, clauses and/or sentences begin and end;
(d) which words are important in the message?

12.6 Look at the way the following words are represented in the spoken utterance above:

NEXT   FOR   THE   SEVEN   FROM   PLATFORM

What are your comments?

Phoneme You are familiar with the term PHONEME, meaning a single contrastive unit of the phonological system of a language. It is 'contrastive' because a phoneme like /k/ serves to distinguish *cat* from *hat* and *rat*; similarly /æ/ distinguishes *cat* from *cut* and *cart*. We sometimes tend to think of a phoneme as if it were a separate and clearly defined unit in the speech stream just as a letter is distinct and physically visible on the page. As we shall see, that is not the case.

PHONEME RECOGNITION

Using a special recording instrument, it is possible to produce a graphic showing exactly what sounds are present in a piece of speech. There are
Spectrograms some examples of these SPECTROGRAMS in Figure 12.1. Vertically, they
Frequencies show what is happening at different FREQUENCIES at any given moment. Horizontally, they show how the speech signal changes over time. The
Intensity dark bands show where there are patches of INTENSITY (loudness). As you can see, they occur at certain frequencies and not at others, and it is these bands of intensity that help to identify a particular sound.

EXERCISE

12.7 Look at Figure 12.1.

(a) Using the spectrograms for KEY and CAR work out which parts of the signal represent consonants and which represent vowels. What differences do you notice?
(b) Look at the spectrograms for CAR and CAT. Can you mark precisely the point where /k/ ends and the vowel begins?

(c) Now compare the /k/ in each of the five spectrograms. Is it the same? Compare the /t/ in the spectrograms for KIT, CAT and CAUGHT.

(d) Say KIT/CAT several times in quick succession. Notice where your tongue is when saying the /k/.

key

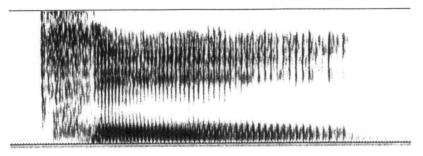

car

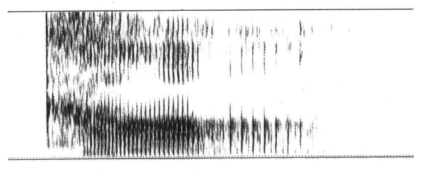

kit

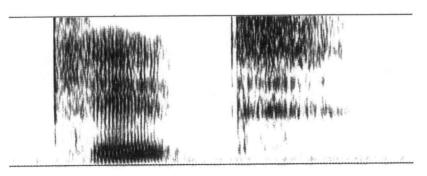

12.1
Spectograms of words that follow the pattern /k/ + vowel + /t/ and /k/ + vowel + /t/

cat

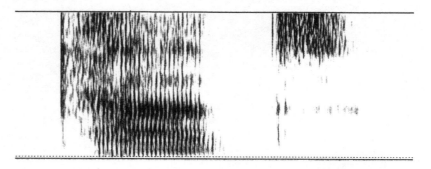

caught

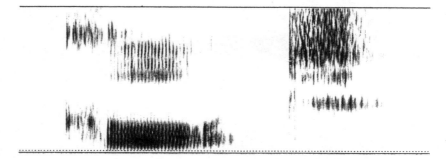

12.1
continued

When studying listening, we have to accept that phonemes in the speech stream:

(a)   vary greatly, because how the speaker says them is heavily influenced by adjoining phonemes in the same syllable.

(b)   blend into each other. One commentator famously suggested that they are not like beads on a string; but much more like the outcome of an accident in an egg packing factory.

So how does a listener manage to recognise the sounds of speech?

EXERCISE

12.8 Look back at page 47 where Prototype Theory is discussed as a way of accounting for the fact that many different types of bird are still identifiable as members of the category BIRD. Does this suggest a possible solution?

Another possible solution is that we do not listen to speech in terms of phonemes at all. We might use a larger unit.

EXERCISE

12.9 Say the following words. Identify the groups of phonemes that occur in more than one word.

> consumption   exciting   reckon   somebody
> Egyptian   physics   tinker

The syllable has been suggested as a possible unit of perception, since whole syllables do not vary in the way that individual phonemes do.

DIFFERENT SPEAKERS

A further problem for theories of listening is that speech varies widely according to the person who is speaking.

EXERCISES

12.10 Consider the ways in which the speech signal might vary:

(a)   according to gender;
(b)   according to age;
(c)   according to where the speaker is from;
(d)   according to the situation: formal or informal;
(e)   according to the speaker's mood (excited, angry, tired, worried).

Which of these are always true of a given speaker, and which might vary from encounter to encounter?

12.11 Decide which of these factors would lead to differences:

- in the pitch of the speaker's voice;
- in how fast the speaker spoke;
- in how loudly the speaker spoke;
- in how often the speaker paused;
- in the phonemes the speaker uttered;
- in the speaker's intonation.

We have a very good memory for speakers' voices. When we hear a speaker for the first time, it is amazing how quickly we manage to adjust (NORMALISE) to the basic pitch and loudness of their voice and to the accent they have. But we also have to show flexibility about factors like SPEECH RATE: the same speaker might speed up when they were enthusiastic about something or slow down to emphasise a point. It seems that listeners monitor speech rate from moment to moment.

Normalise

Speech rate

LOCATING WORDS

Look again at the sample of spoken language that we studied above:

thəneckstrainfəLONdən + isthəsebmFORtyfrəmpla'form
EIGHT +

In connected speech, there are no regular gaps between the words. So how does the listener manage to work out where words begin and end? One answer was provided in Unit 8 by Cohort Theory. In principle, the listener waits until a word is complete (has reached its uniqueness point); then assumes that a new word is about to begin.

EXERCISES

12.12 How would this technique work with this piece of speech?

thecaptain'sincabinsixteen.

12.13 Use the phoneme table at the beginning of this book to work out the meaning of the following pieces of speech.

(a) /ðə|weitə|kʌtit/
(b) /|wentʊə|sistə/
(c) /ə|tæksɒnðə|piːpəl/
(d) /|wiːkən|fast/

Now say how your answer would change if the adjacent words were:

(a)   . . . with a knife   . . . is like this
(b)   . . . of John's   . . . in carrying her luggage
(c)   . . . were resisted   . . . is unfair
(d)   . . . to lose weight   He will . . . without medicine.
       An athlete can't be . . .

Listeners face a problem of LEXICAL SEGMENTATION – deciding where word boundaries lie. They may sometimes have to carry two possible interpretations in their head until the context tells them which is the correct one.

Lexical segmentation

However, there is evidence that English-speaking listeners often choose one interpretation as the preferred one. They take advantage of the fact that around 90 per cent of content words in running speech are either monosyllabic or begin with a stressed syllable. So there is a high likelihood that a new word will begin at each stressed syllable. This seems to be the assumption that they make when dividing up the speech stream. They attach unstressed syllables to the stressed ones that precede them.

EXERCISE

12.14 How would this segmentation strategy work with our sample piece of speech?

> thəneckstrainfəLONdən + isthəsebmFORtyfrəmpla'form EIGHT +

bold type = stressed syllable   bold type plus CAPS = heavy stress

What preferred interpretation would it give for the examples (a) to (d) in Exercise 12.13?

Not all languages pose this lexical segmentation problem for the listener; indeed, English may be untypical.

EXERCISE

12.15 English has the problem because its LEXICAL STRESS varies from word to word. Say the following words aloud, and decide how they vary in stress

Lexical stress

> photograph   photographic   photography

In many other languages, lexical stress falls consistently on a given syllable of a content word:

- In Hungarian and Czech, stress is always on the first syllable.
- In Persian, stress is always on the last syllable (except for prefixed verbs).

- In Bahasa Indonesia, stress is always on the penultimate syllable.

Suggest how this would assist lexical segmentation.

PROJECT

Gating

Make use of a method known as GATING. Record a piece of natural connected speech – perhaps somebody speaking informally on the radio. Choose four sentences from your recording, each of about 7 or 8 words. Now edit the sentences using a tape-recorder or (better still) a computer program. Produce a recording for each sentence which consists of:

> 'Gate' 1: the first word of the sentence followed by a pause (about 6 seconds);
> 'Gate' 2: the first two words of the sentence followed by the same pause;
> 'Gate' 3: the first three words of the sentence followed by the same pause;

and so on.

Play your edited recording to subjects and ask them during the pauses to write down what they have heard. Use around 10 subjects. Compare their answers to see how successfully they recognise words that have been taken out of a sentence context.

Then for each word, note the gate at which it is first successfully identified. It may be the gate where it first appeared or it may be a later one. In particular, compare how quickly listeners identify: (a) function words as against content words; (b) short content words as against long ones.

For use with Exercise 11.12.

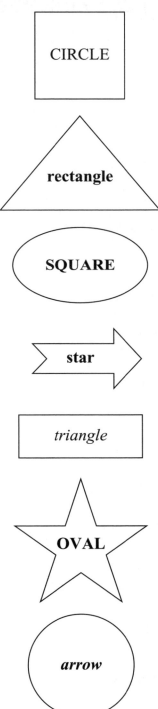

ANSWERS TO EXERCISES

UNIT 1 LANGUAGE AND ANIMALS

1.1 *Speech*: the oral form of language. It involves vocalisation (i.e. making sounds).

Language: a system of grammar and vocabulary and a system of **Modality** pronunciation and writing. It includes both MODALITIES (spoken and written); it includes receptive skills (listening, reading) as well as productive ones (speaking, writing).

Communication: a means of transmitting information. Includes language and other means of transmission such as facial expressions, gestures, mime etc.

1.2 (a) Indexical

(b) Symbolic

(c) Symbolic

(d) Possibly indexical; possibly iconic

(e) Symbolic

(f) Iconic or indexical

1.3 It is different from language because it is not voluntary: the chimp is not able to suppress it when he wants to. It is a kind of reflex action, like laughing or flinching.

1.4 1 (d); 2 (f); 3 (h); 4 (e); 5 (g); 6 (c); 7 (b); 8 (a).

1.5 * **Vervet monkeys**

(a) *Similarities to language.* The alarm calls are *arbitrary*. They enable *displacement* because vervets that have not seen the threat hear and repeat the calls. The calls appear to have *semanticity*.

Distinct calls refer to distinct concepts, so they could be described as symbolic. But the three threats come from three different directions. So the 'bird of prey' call may not refer specifically to a bird of prey but to a threat from the sky.

(b) *Differences*. Vervet monkeys only have a limited repertoire of vocal sounds compared with speech. The calls are complete units which do not vary. They do not have *dual patterning* or *creativity*.

The call is picked up and echoed by other vervets; this is not the same as saying that they reply to the call. So there is no *interchangeability*. Finally, on *control*, the account does not make clear whether the calls are voluntary; they might be reflexive responses to danger.

* Worker bees

(a) *Similarities to language*. The bees use their dances in ways that show *semanticity* (a different dance for a different message). The dances also achieve *displacement*: referring to something that is not present. The dances are *arbitrary* in the way they indicate distance but are indexical in the way they indicate direction.

(b) *Differences*. The range of signals is very limited, and the ideas they convey are restricted to distance and forward direction (there is no way of indicating 'up' and 'down'). There is no *creativity*.

The flow of information is one-way, so there is no *interchangeability*. And, as the dances are innate, they are not *culturally transmitted* and might well be *reflexive*.

* Dolphins

(a) *Similarities to language*. Dolphins have a whole system of clicks, so we can assume that they have *semanticity* (different clicks for different information). The clicks are also clearly *arbitrary*. The clicks enable *displacement* – giving information to dolphins that are a long way away from the food source. They may or may not be under the dolphins' voluntary *control*.

(b) *Differences*. The account says that evidence is unclear about whether the system has *interchangeability*. It does not say whether different signals can be combined in ways that would give *creativity*.

1.6 The dog has not really 'acquired' the word. Most obviously, it cannot use the word spontaneously itself. It has formed an association between the string of sounds and an event. But if WALK is said on several occasions but no walk ensues, then the association will be broken. In other words, there is no inevitable symbolic connection in the mind of the dog.

1.7 The parrot has learnt by a process of STIMULUS (owner takes cover off; owner says *Good morning*) – RESPONSE (parrot imitates) – REWARD (nuts). But that does not mean that it has learnt the concept of MORNING – only that it associates the whole phrase with the removal of the cover, which could happen at any time of day. And if the nuts were not forthcoming, it might soon stop performing and the connection between cover and phrase would be broken.

1.8 Kanzi achieved some kind of symbolic use of language since the association between the computer keys and the objects/actions they referred to was *arbitrary*. At five years old and after much training, he had a vocabulary of 400 symbols. But this is far fewer than a human child of that age. Furthermore, he could only produce a limited set of two-word combinations; a human infant achieves this at around 2 years old. On the other hand, it means that some *dual patterning* and some *creativity* was present. Apparently, there was also interchangeability since Kanzi could both produce and understand utterances. But we have to bear in mind that this was not the normal initiation-response of conversation and that the exchanges were in two different forms (the trainers using speech and Kanzi using keyboard symbols).

   The most important issue is whether Kanzi fully appreciated the symbolic nature of language. There is some evidence that he did, in that he was able to group symbols into larger categories. On the other hand, there is a big question as to whether his use of language was entirely voluntary. To what extent was he expressing himself and to what extent was communication directed towards gaining food and comfort from his trainers?

UNIT 2 LANGUAGE AND THE BRAIN

2.1 (a)   The elephant and the whale have larger brains.

   (b)   The brains of rodents are much more densely packed with neurons (because they are so small).

   (c)   The ratio of brain to body size is up to twice as great in mice as it is in human beings.

   (d)   This is the right answer. Our body increases in weight at very much the same pace as other primates. But our brain increases in weight at a rate that one would expect in a much larger mammal such as a dolphin.

2.2 (a)   The larger cortex of human beings equips them for locating stored information like words, syntactic patterns and world knowledge. It also helps them to make quick connections between these items.

(b) Human beings have much greater control over the organs that they need in order to utter speech. In most mammals, the motor areas control movements of the mouth, tongue and lips, but the movements concerned are for the purposes of eating and grooming rather than uttering calls.

(c) The larger cerebellum gives human beings greater scope to coordinate the automatic movements involved in stringing together the sounds of speech.

(d) Greater voluntary control over the larynx enables human beings to coordinate breathing and speaking. In other species, the larynx mainly operates as part of a reflex action that prevents food from getting into the windpipe.

2.3 Many of the motor operations performed by right-handed human beings are controlled by the left hemisphere; while those performed by left-handed individuals are controlled by the right. As we will see, there appears to be some connection between language and handedness. Although for most people the left hemisphere is the more important one for language, some left-handed people have a right-hemisphere dominance.

(a) A message played to the right ear would be processed by the left hemisphere of the brain.

(b) It might seem that a word that was shown to the left eye would be processed by the right hemisphere of the brain. In fact, the eyes work rather like the body as a whole. The left field of vision in each eye connects to the right hemisphere of the brain, while the right field of vision connects to the left hemisphere.

2.4 The research suggests that the preferred hemisphere for processing language is the left one. The numbers heard by the left ear and processed by the right hemisphere were not given the same level of attention.

2.5 The patient suffering from Broca's aphasia:

- cannot construct sentences (i.e. has problems of syntax) and as a result speaks very hesitantly;
- uses very few function words such as *the, in, with, of*;
- appears to recognise that certain words exist but has trouble in retrieving them. He produces *steps* instead of 'stool' and *cof* instead of 'cloth'.

The patient suffering from Wernicke's aphasia:

- speaks fluently with few hesitations, but repeats words (*made made made*);
- constructs quite complex sentences (*they've got something which is made*) and uses syntactic patterns (*seems to have got*);

- has difficulty in retrieving the vocabulary that he needs and sometimes seems to have lost any connections that would enable him to find words. He uses vague words such as *something, woman, stuff*;
- has trouble constructing sequences of words that represent the meaning he wants to put across;

Formulaic chunks

- but seems to have retained the kind of FORMULAIC CHUNKS of language that people use a lot, sometimes with very little meaning: *it's just beginning to, go and be, I'm rather surprised that, but there you are, one and another, I suppose the idea is that, should be fairly good* and *as I say*. This gives his speech the appearance of being more meaningful than it is.

2.6 Figure 2.1 shows that there is a greater likelihood that a left-handed person will have right-hemisphere dominance for language or will have no dominant hemisphere. But the majority of left-handed people are left-hemisphere dominant.

Figure 2.2 shows that there is some evidence that language re-later-alises after damage to the left hemisphere early in life. It only happens in a minority of cases where the sufferer is right-handed. But it seems to happen frequently when the sufferer is left-handed.

The fact is that, overall, re-lateralisation does not happen as consistently as was once assumed.

2.7 (a)   Figure 2.3 suggests that language is very widely distributed in the brain and not just localised in the Broca and Wernicke areas.

(b)   They might simply be involved in a lot of language operations (even if these operations also involve many other parts of the brain). Or they might be major 'crossroads' which are critical in the transmission of linguistic information from one part of the brain to another.

2.8 (a)   Listening to the phonology of speech is very demanding because we have to listen at different levels. On the one hand, we need to listen for small units (phonemes) which are articulated very rapidly. On the other hand, we have to listen for large intonation patterns extending over several syllables. Perhaps lateralisation results from the need to keep these two operations apart.

Discourse

(b)   A similar case can be made for separating the processing of details of grammar (including small-scale units like inflections which need to be recognised rapidly) from the processing of larger patterns of DISCOURSE such as the structure of a narrative.

UNIT 3   LANGUAGE AND THE GRAMMAR GENE

3.1 (a)   The pigeon was trained to follow the rules of table tennis but it did not know what it was doing. It simply adopted certain behaviour patterns because it expected a reward afterwards in the form of food. As we saw with the examples of animal training in Unit 2, that is very different from acquiring a language. A language is *meaningful*: it involves the transmission of information that reflects the speaker's own immediate thoughts, wishes and needs. A language is also extremely *complex* compared with knocking a ball over a net.

(b)   It is stretching the behaviourist theory rather far. Why exactly is an object in the real world a stimulus? And why does it necessarily call forth a response in the form of the child uttering the word that names it?

(c)   No, they tend to correct facts, but they do not tend to correct language.

(d)   Yes, they do, and this is an important means of learning the phonology of the language. But infants often parrot what an adult says (even chunks of two or three words) without fully understanding it and certainly without internalising its grammar.

(e)   Much of the time the parents may be engaging in Baby Talk which is not very representative of normal language: *Who's a clever girl then?*

3.2   At 2;4 (note the way we show two years and four months), Sophie uses simple subject + verb sequences (*daddy come down*). She uses the object form *me* instead of the subject form *I*. She does not inflect the verb *come* to make it agree with *Daddy*. She cannot use the more complex PROGRESSIVE form used by her mother (*Daddy is coming down*). **Progressive**

At 3;0 Sophie can form past questions with *do* (*Why did you give her?*). She knows that she must follow *did* with the stem of the verb (*give*, not the past form *gave*). She can even form NEGATIVE QUESTIONS: *Why didn't me get flu?* She still has problems with subject pronouns (*her been flu*) and with inflected forms of irregular verbs (*been* for *was*). **Negative questions**

At 3;11, Sophie is more fluent, as seen in her longer sentences. Her sentences are also more complex (*he say if you push that thing again*). Some of her past tenses are accurate, though she still has problems with *say* and the less frequent *flied*. She knows how to use general terms when she does not know a piece of vocabulary (*pointy thing*). She has also picked up the conversational 'filler' *you see*. Here, she may well have imitated adults.

3.3 The mother supplies support for the child's vocabulary. But she does not correct the child's grammar as behaviourist theory would suggest, and is clearly not training her to form grammatical habits. Note, though, that she does talk in grammatically correct sentences, thus indirectly giving the child a model.

3.4 One of the remarkable aspects of language learning is that almost every child acquires the complex grammatical system of its first language in the first 6 or 7 years of life, regardless of the child's intelligence in performing other activities. Less able children may end up with a limited vocabulary, but they achieve full grammatical competence.

3.5 This adult language does not provide a clear model because it has hesitations, false starts (where the speaker changes the format of what he intends to say) and repetitions. It even has some structures that might strike one as ungrammatical (*it was a blizzard on*). Like much conversational speech, it is strung together loosely by the word *and*, so it does not provide a model of more complex sentences with subordinate clauses. This extract provides an example of language performance. It is difficult to see how a child could get behind the performance and work out the underlying grammar rules.

3.6 (a) [My aunt and uncle] [[bought a house] [with the money]].

with the money is subordinate to *bought a house*. We could show it like this:

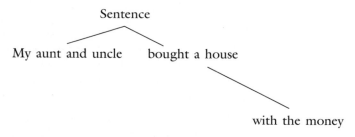

(b) [The old man [with the long beard]] [was reading] [a newspaper].

with the long beard is subordinate to *the old man*

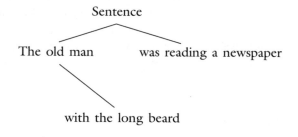

3.7 In English, speakers have to use a pronoun subject. But in Italian, the pronoun subject can be dropped. Languages like Italian use an inflection at the end of the verb (*parlo – parli – parla*) to show who or what the subject is.

3.8 (a) It might show that UG dictates the order in which the features of the language are acquired. Or the child might start off by acquiring features that are part of UG because they are common to all languages.

(b) The age ranges are quite complicated to compare. First, it would appear that there is quite a lot of overlap between the different features. This makes it difficult to say with certainty that one comes before another. Today, commentators tend to present these features in groups with (e.g.), *-ing, in/on* and *-s* plural shown as likely to occur early on. Second, it is interesting to note how wide the age ranges are. For irregular past forms, there was 11 months difference between the earliest and the latest child. This illustrates a very important point: *that there is enormous variation in the rates at which children acquire the grammar of their language.*

(c) The order in which these features are acquired might simply reflect the fact that some of them are more difficult to grasp than others. This would explain why the article (*a* and *the*) comes quite late. The relative frequency of the items does not seem to be a factor. If it were, we might expect *a* and *the* to be acquired first. But it is just possible that the order of acquisition is influenced by how perceptible these items are. It is quite easy to hear *-ing, in* and *on*; but (e.g.), *a* and *the* are usually said in a weak form that is quite difficult to hear.

(d) This is a problem. Brown decided that a feature was 'acquired' if it was accurately used 90 per cent of the time. But it is not always easy to tell whether a child is fully aware of the function of any feature that it is using. For example, the child might use plural words like *ears* or *eyes* as items of vocabulary, without fully realising that they have a singular form.

UNIT 4 LANGUAGE AND THE CHILD

4.1 (a) Possible answers include:

Phonology: higher pitched voice – slower speech – some words are 'stretched' – increased stress – simple intonation patterns.

Grammar: simple grammar – lots of questions (even when the adults know the answers) – utterances often repeated two or three times – a few basic grammar structures used frequently.

Lexis: many nouns (names of visible objects) – words that are frequent in everyday speech – some baby words (*diddums*).

(b)   Possible answers are:

Simplifying: simple intonation – simple grammar – frequent use of same grammar pattern – frequent vocabulary.

Clarifying: slower speech – 'stretched' words – increased stress – utterances often repeated – use of nouns (visible objects).

Expressing feelings: higher pitched voice – baby words.

(c)   Many adults appear to adjust their speech – introducing more complex grammar and less frequent words as the child gets older.

4.2   (a)   The utterances in CDS are much shorter than in normal speech. There are many more isolated phrases. But much of CDS seems to consist of complete sentences that are grammatically correct. At 60 per cent, this is about the same proportion as in speech to adults. Even the isolated phrases are mainly correct.

(b)   CDS seems to be better-formed than Chomsky suggested.

(c)   There are more imperatives in CDS. We might expect this since parents are likely to encourage and reprove a child (*Behave!*). But there are also many more questions. This seems to show a wish by parents to encourage the child to communicate, a more important function of CDS than conveying information via declarative sentences. There is also (not shown separately in the table) much use of TAG QUESTIONS: *It's nice, isn't it*? *You ate it all, didn't you?*. Again, such questions encourage participation.

Tag questions

(d)   The many questions in CDS have another value in that they allow the child to hear AUXILIARY VERBS (*is* and *have*) which are shortened (CONTRACTED) in ordinary declarative sentences and so are barely audible. In the case of *do/does/did*, we only use the auxiliary verb in the question (cf. *He broke a glass/Did he break a glass?*). Children often pick up *Did you?/Do you?/Does he?* as CHUNKS which help them to form their own questions.

Auxillary verbs
Contracted

Chunks

Deixis

4.3   Note the much higher proportion of CDS that involves DEIXIS. The parent names objects in the child's environment and describes how they are placed in relation to where the child is sitting. In this way, the child learns new vocabulary and acquires spatial awareness.

There is a little self-repetition in adult speech – though a good lecturer might make the same point two or three times to emphasise it. But a striking 23 per cent of CDS involves REPETITION of some kind – ensuring that the child understands the message.

Repetition

Adult carers sometimes repeat sentences produced by the child (mainly correct ones) or rephrase (RECAST) them to make them clearer or more

Recast

accurate. This rarely happens with adult-to-adult conversation. These EXPANSIONS serve the function of adding new forms of language to the child's repertoire. At a given stage of development, a child might chiefly produce two-word utterances. Expansions demonstrate how it can, in time, extend them into three- and four-word utterances.

Expansions

4.4 (a)   The adult turns in the conversation are as follows:

Line 2   The mother rephrases, demonstrating a useful grammatical pattern (*in the stomach*). The mother adds a reassuring chunk (*yes that's right*) showing understanding.

Line 4   The mother rephrases, adding an *–ing* inflection. She extends what the child says, making it coherent with what has gone before. She adds a tag question, encouraging a response from the child. Note how the child then echoes the new phrase *on our pancakes*.

Line 6   The mother asks a question, keeping the conversation going by giving it a new direction. She simplifies the question, using an ordinary affirmative sentence but with a question intonation. This is the first question form that many infants use; and the mother may be adjusting what she says to take account of the child's own language. Note how the mother echoes the *on our pancakes* phrase that the child has just picked up.

Line 8   It's not clear that the mother has understood the child's meaning. But she rephrases what the child said and keeps the conversation going. She also adds a tag question.

Line 10   The child's two-word utterance is comprehensible. But the father expands it into a better formed four-word one.

Line 12   The father keeps the conversation going: he makes use of previous key words (*daddy, pancakes*).

Line 14   The father recasts and extends the unclear 2- and 3-word utterances of the child. Note how he recasts *in plate* as *on your plate*, without specifically correcting the child.

4.5 (a)   Slower speech and more pausing help the infant to recognise words (there are no consistent pauses between words in speech like those in writing). Heavy stress and lengthened syllables help the child to hear which are the most important words in the utterance and to separate them out from the others. When pauses and syllable lengthening happen at the end of a clause, they mark out the grammar patterns in what is being said. Increased pausing might also give the child time to 'catch up' on what has been said so far.

(b)   High pitch level holds the child's attention. It might also be a way in which the adult shows empathy with the child by imitating the child's own voice.

4.6 Their innate Universal Grammar might tell them that words exist.
They might pick up words (e.g. names) in isolation, then recognise them in continuous speech.
They might recognise strings of sounds that occur quite often.

4.7 Infants seem to assume that all words begin with a stressed syllable (in fact, most words in running English speech do). So they ignore the first syllable of *giraffe* and *banana* but reproduce *monkey* accurately.

4.8 BOON – CAmel – NOcerous – RILla – Elephant – POTamus – QUIto – PORcupine

4.9 They noticed a minimal difference between two common sentence patterns:

A It's . . .   B It's a . . .

They probably noticed first that proper names they had come across (including their own name) were used in Pattern A. Objects pointed out to them by their carers (i.e. common nouns) were used in Pattern B.
Next, they must have recognised that where an object had an overall permanent shape (and could be picked up singly), it was used in Pattern B, while shapeless objects (*sugar*, *water*) were used in Pattern A. A similar explanation accounts for the child's ability to form a plural: it recognises a minimal difference between a word such as *cup* applied to a single item that it picks up and *cups* applied to more than one.

UNIT 5   LANGUAGE AND DISADVANTAGE

5.1   aphasia after an accident: acquired language impairment
language acquisition by a deaf child: exceptional circumstances
autism: developmental language impairment
the language of twins: exceptional circumstances
stuttering: developmental gap in competence/performance
the effects of a stroke: acquired language impairment
dyslexia: developmental gap in competence
Downs Syndrome: developmental language impairment
depriving a young child of language: exceptional circumstances

5.2   1 *get* → cet   Wrong sound–spelling relationship, or mishearing? F
2 *oxygen* → oschun   Missed out a syllable.   B
3 *else* → esle   Letters in wrong order.   G
4 *father* → fther   Letter missed out.   D

5 *squeezing* → scweecing   Correct sound *scw-*; wrong spelling. E

6 *daddy* → baddy   Reversed the *d*. C

7 *language* → languaguage   Repeated a syllable. A

Target	Spelling	Type	Target	Spelling	Type	Target	Spelling	Type
first	firsk	F	because	deakos	C E	ropes	roaps	E
exceptionally	explunaly	B	people	pepeole	G	damage	damageage	A
odd numbers	obd nudners	C	baby	baybiy	E	suddenly	suddly	B
departure	depacher	E	pudding	pubbing	C	forty	fortyty	A
army	amry	G	different	diffent	B	examined	igzamind	E
negotiations	nocosiatios	E	square	sqaurare	A	two	tow	G

5.3   A form   B sound   C form   D sound   E form   F form (wrong sound–spelling relationship) or sound   G form

E suggests that the writer has a clear idea of the sound–spelling relationship but is not using it accurately in working out how to spell words.

5.4   Subject A: surface

Subject B: surface

Subject C: phonological

Subject D: either surface or phonological

Subject E: surface

Subject F: phonological

Subject G: surface

Subject H: phonological

Subject I: surface

5.5   *Vocabulary:* she uses simple words: almost all are one-syllable. She only uses very frequent words. Her vocabulary seems to be small but accurate.

Syntax: her grammar is incomplete. She has correct word order. But her sentences are very short (2–5 words). She does not use function words (*a, the, of, on, with* etc.). She does not inflect for past tense (*Father take* for *Father took*) though she uses *is* correctly. She does not even form the negative imperative correctly (*Not spit* for *Don't spit*). But she has one quite complex structure *Father make me cry*.

5.6   (a)   Genie was 13 when she was found – well into adolescence and thus beyond the limits that are put on the critical period. She achieved limited vocabulary but did not achieve full language competence.

(b) Genie cannot be said to be a typical case. She was not a healthy child, and possibly had learning problems. Her mental development may have been damaged by the way she was treated; this may also have damaged her ability or wish to interact socially. The left hemisphere of her brain may have been damaged.

We should also note that Genie's language advanced when she was given care and attention but stopped when she became insecure. This might support a view of language as (in part at least) dependent upon social interaction. It is possible too that (as some adult second language learners do) she stopped bothering to acquire new language once she had enough to make her needs and wishes clear.

(c) Genie's general cognitive development seemed to advance faster than her language.

5.7 *Evidence supporting modularity:* Williams Syndrome, Christopher the savant, Specific Language Impairment

Evidence against modularity: Downs Syndrome, autism (though the problems in autism may be social as well as cognitive).

UNIT 6 STORING WORDS

6.1 *With lexical meaning* (content words) DRIVE FATHER SLOW MUST NEVER BELONG FIGHT NASTY SUGAR LONDON

Without lexical meaning (function words) A TO BUT IT WHEN SO THAT

With some lexical meaning (prepositions of position) IN BEHIND

Problematic word: MICHAEL, a name which does not have lexical meaning

6.2 Each group of words forms a single lexical entry because they represent a single idea. Because of groups like this, it is often better to refer to lexical items rather than words; the term includes one-word and multi-word items.

6.3 The best solution is to envisage HEAVY and SMOKER as two separate entries that are very closely connected in the lexicon. So when we retrieve SMOKER, we also make contact with HEAVY.

6.4 (b) seems more efficient: i.e. we add on inflections when we need them. After all, inflectional suffixes do not change the central meaning of the word; they just show its grammatical function within the sentence.

6.5 This is more difficult. Derivational prefixes and suffixes actually create new words (with new dictionary meanings); Solution (a) recognises this by giving them their own entries. Solution (b) would seem more efficient but remember that entries in the lexicon usually carry lexical meaning. What exactly is the meaning of -NESS?

6.6 Here is a problem for Solution (b). It is not enough just to have a set of word roots and a set of prefixes that are added to them. We need to add DIS- to HONEST, MIS- to UNDERSTAND and DE- to MOTI-VATE – just as we add UN- to HAPPY. We have to assume that there is a close connection between the entry for HAPPY and the entry for UN-, preventing us from making a wrong connection with DIS- or MIS-when we assemble the opposite. This is rather like the link we assumed between SMOKER and HEAVY.

6.7 (a)   A listener would break UNCERTAIN into UN + CERTAIN. He/she could then locate the root of the word (CERTAIN) in order to obtain its meaning. The prefix UN- (= not) would then modify that meaning. Other pieces of prefix-stripping: DIS + APPEAR, MIS + MANAGE, IN + EFFICIENT.

(b)   A problem for the prefix-splitting account. We have to assume that, every time a listener hears a prefix-like sequence, they automatically strip it off to get to the root of the word. But this does not work with UN + DERSTAND (or UNDER + STAND), with DIS + APPOINT, with MIS + TAKE or with IN + FORM. Granted, the listener arrives at roots that are actual words, but they do not help us to understand the meaning of the whole item: what has TAKE to do with MISTAKE or STAND with UNDER-STAND?

6.8 *Could be two entries:* RE + NAME, RE + CONSIDER, RE + WRITE, RE + BUILD, RE + PRINT

Could not be two entries: REVISE, RETURN, REFRESH, RECOVER, REPLY, REPAIR, RENEW, REMIND.

6.9 You need information about:

(a)   the word's spelling;

(b)   the way it inflects to show past time (WROTE);

(c)   its meaning (as compared with the meanings of other similar words);

(d)   the kind of grammar pattern it appears in (e.g. *write a . . . to . . . .*)

6.10 (a)   AFRAID

Form: spelling: A-F-R-A-I-D   pronunciation: /əˈfreɪd/
           morphology: *more afraid – most afraid*

Lemma: meaning: fearful
           differs from meanings of: FRIGHTENED –
           TERRIFIED – NERVOUS
           word-class: adjective
           syntactic pattern: be + AFRAID + *of*

(b)   SHOW

Form: spelling: S-H-O-W   pronunciation: /ʃəʊ/
           morphology: *showed – shown – showing*

Lemma: meaning: display
           differs from meanings of: DEMONSTRATE – REVEAL
           – EXHIBIT
           word-class: verb
           syntactic pattern: SHOW + something + *to* + somebody
                              SHOW + somebody + something

(c)   PUT

Form: spelling: P-U-T   pronunciation: /pʊt/
           morphology: *put – put – putting*

Lemma: meaning: place
           differs from meanings of: LOCATE – POSITION –
           INSERT
           word-class: verb
           syntactic pattern: PUT + something + *in/on/under* +
           receptacle

6.11 (a)   A building used for domestic habitation and not subdivided.

(b)   A BUNGALOW is a house with only one floor. A COTTAGE is a small house in the country. A MANSION is a large house with many rooms. But an APARTMENT is not a house at all: it is a living space which is part of a larger building and usually on one floor of that building.

6.12 Rated close to 1 are likely to be: bed, table, wardrobe, armchair, bookshelf. Rated closer to 16 are likely to be: computer, carpet, radiator, cooker, vase.

6.13 1 has wings, flies   2 sings   3 has feathers   4 builds a nest in a tree   5 lays eggs   6 quite small in size   7 eats corn, worms, insects

Close to prototype: SPARROW, THRUSH, CANARY

Quite close: HAWK (meat eating), DUCK (on water), OWL (nocturnal), PARROT (no singing)

Distant: OSTRICH (bald in parts, no flying, large, no song), PENGUIN (upright, no flying, no song)

Outside the category: BAT

6.14 Rosch's subjects may have chosen their typical items because they were the most *frequent* or the most *familiar* ones in their environment. The choice may have been affected by *culture* (ROBIN was high for Americans, perhaps because of Christmas cards). Very different proto-types might be chosen by people from other environments and cultures. Example: for Africans, PARROT or FLAMINGO might rate highly among birds and YAM among vegetables.

UNIT 7   FINDING WORDS

7.1   (a)   A listener is presented with the *spoken form* of a word. She has to match that to a mental representation of how the word is pronounced. In this way, she locates the lexical entry and finds out the *meaning* of the word.

(b)   A writer has a *meaning* that he wants to express. He also prob-ably has a sense that a given word exists. He has to use the meaning to locate the word in his mental lexicon. Then he has to retrieve the *written form* of the word. The writer also needs to know the word-class of the word, the syntactic patterns that it appears in etc.

(c)   Like the writer, a speaker has a *meaning* that she wants to express and a sense that an appropriate word exists. She uses the meaning to locate the word and then has to retrieve the *spoken form* of the word. This has to be done very fast, whereas the writer has time to reflect on whether the word chosen is the right one. The speaker also needs to know the word-class of the word, the syntactic patterns that it appears in etc.

7.2   SPINACH: vegetables. Other members: CABBAGE, SPROUTS, BROCCOLI, PEAS, BEANS, CARROTS etc. The set may be different in other languages (e.g. Spanish).

HAMMER: tools. Other members: SCREWDRIVER, CHISEL, SAW etc.

To MARCH: ways of walking. Other members: STROLL, WANDER, HURRY, STRUT, LIMP etc.

CUPBOARD: household furniture. Other members: CHAIR, TABLE, BOOKSHELF, BED, RUG etc.

TAXI: (public) transport. Other members: BUS, TRAIN, PLANE, SHIP etc.

HUGE: largeness. Other members: BIG, LARGE, ENORMOUS, MASSIVE etc.

To FETCH: moving an object. Other members: BRING, TAKE etc.

COAT: clothing. Other members: SCARF, DRESS, SUIT, SHIRT, SKIRT etc.

7.3 The important thing is the experience of doing the task. The answers are:

(a) cicada   (b) aviary   (c) psychosomatic
(d) ostracise   (e) truism, cliché (f) desecrate
(g) submersible   (h) articulated   (i) mangrove

Compare the words you produced with the correct ones. How close were they?

7.4 (a)   architectural features (inside).

(b)   Its form (spoken or written); its word-class; its morphology (plural in −*s*) how it contrasts with other similar words.

(c)   It is very similar to BANNISTER, the correct word. Compare the first and last syllable.

7.5 (a)   Same first syllable; same number of syllables; same stress on first syllable.

(b)   Same last syllable (in *porcupine*, last two syllables are very similar; in *anonymously*, last three syllables are the same); same number of syllables; same stress pattern.

(c)   Same first and last syllables; same number of syllables; same stress pattern.

(d)   Same consonants in the same place; same number of syllables; same stress pattern.

(e)   The speaker has chosen two words with similar meanings: MOSTLY and MAINLY and has produced a combination of the two. The speaker seems to be using the first syllable as a cue to the word.

7.6 (a)   SIGH, SIGN, SIGHT, SILENT, SIMON, SCIENCE, CIDER, CYCLE, CYPHER, CYBERSPACE, PSYCHOLOGY, ETC.

(b)   You will have kept: CYCLE, CYCLIST, PSYCHOLOGY, PSYCHOTIC, PSYCHIATRIC, etc.

(c)   PSYCHOLOGY

7.7 (a)   With each of these words, we would identify a wrong target word before the word was actually complete: READ in *reading*, ENTER in *entertain*, YOU in *unity*.

(b)   We can divide these sequences up in two different ways: SENT A PAGE/CENTRE PAGE, THE WAY TO CUT IT/THE WAITER CUT IT. So we do not just need to match words; we also need to work out where they begin and end.

(c)   The listener would construct a cohort of words beginning with *shi-* SHIP, SHIFT, SHILLING, SHIMMER etc. The cohort would not include the word CIGARETTE because the original Cohort Theory is critically dependent upon the first syllable of a word being heard correctly.

7.8 *Activated*: PROFESSION, PROFESSOR. *Less activated*: PROWESS, PROGRESS, PROCESSOR. *Weakly activated*: PROMISE, CONFESSION, PREFERS (some letters the same). *Very weak*: FOREST. *Negative activation*: MAXIMUM, BALANCE

7.9 *Easily recognised*: INCOME, INDEED, INFORM, INJURE, INSECT, INSERT, INSIDE, INSIST, INTEND, INVENT, INVITE. These are the words that occur most frequently in everyday speech and writing.

7.10 HAND LUGGAGE: links to CHECK IN and CABIN

NOSE: links to WINGS, ENGINE and TAIL

BOARDING PASS: links to CHECK IN and BOARD

STEWARDESS: links to CABIN CREW

GATE: links to BOARD

7.11 (a)   Both are colours.

(b)   SPARROW is a type of BIRD.

(c)   FISH often occurs together with CHIPS joined by the word *and*.

(d)   EMPTY is the opposite of FULL.

(e)   KNIFE and FORK are part of a lexical set (cutlery). They also often occur together, joined by *and*.

(f)   A WING is part of a PLANE.

(g)   CLOCK and WATCH belong to the same lexical set (time-pieces).

(h)   VEGETABLE is the class of items to which CARROT belongs.

(i)   If you BUY something from Bill, he SELLS it to you (so BUY is not quite the 'opposite' of SELL).

(j)   FIND has (almost) the same meaning as DISCOVER.

7.12 (a)   A and B belong to the same lexical set;

(b)   A is a hyponym of B;

(c)   A is a collocate of B;

(d)   A is an antonym of B;

(e)   A and B belong to the same lexical set. They are also collocates;

(f)   A is a meronym of B;

(g)   A and B belong to the same lexical set;

(h)   A is a superordinate of B;

(i)   A is the converse of B;

(j)   A is a synonym of B.

UNIT 8   THE WRITING PROCESS

8.1   The first text is simple and informal. It even uses contractions (*don't*). But it has:

* complete and well-formed sentences;
* complex sentences consisting of a main clause and subordinate clause (*unless you are absolutely sure . . .*);
* precise vocabulary (*the caller, enter into any conversation, replace the handset*).

The second text has:

* incomplete and loosely structured sentences;
* many false starts (where the speaker starts a sentence then changes her mind);
* idiomatic formulae (*the thing is*);
* fillers (*kind of, you know*) which give the speaker time to plan ahead;
* non-standard grammar (*what you doing*).

(a)   These differences partly reflect the different conditions under which speech and writing are produced. Writers have time to think, revise and polish what they produce. Speaking, however, is spontaneous and speakers are under time pressure to respond promptly to those they are conversing with. That is why they often fall back on formulaic sequences, rethink what they want to say and make use of fillers to give themselves more time to plan. That is also why speech has a loose structure (stringing together ideas by using *and* and *so*), whereas there are often much more complex syntactic patterns in writing – the result of having time to plan and polish what to say.

(b)   A speaker often knows the listener(s) quite well and, very importantly, can learn a lot about the way they respond to what is said. Indeed, much speaking is interactive, and heavily dependent upon feedback from listeners. Writers have to learn to do without that feedback. They have to make very careful judgements as to who the readers are likely to be and how these readers are likely to interpret (or misinterpret) the piece of writing.

Finally, speakers often have evidence around them that they can refer to, whereas writers usually have to put across a situation or describe objects that are not present to the reader.

8.2   (a)   The ad will need to use language with positive connotations (*deep*, *rich*, *aroma* etc.). But it will also want to appeal to the intelligence of the reader; it will avoid language that is too idiomatic and reminiscent of the tabloid press (*Wow! Strewth!*). Much thought will be given to visual presentation (including the kind of typeface that is used).

(b)   The good professor will feel free to use technical terminology and to assume that quite a lot of his background knowledge is shared with his readers. He will probably conform to certain conventions that we expect in academic texts: an introduction, a review of what other people have written, a presentation of his methods, an analysis of his findings and a conclusion. In this, he recognises the type of discourse that his readers expect.

(c)   Sharon will write in a rather formal style, and may well feel the need to appeal to the self-importance of the councillor. She will support her assertions with examples. She may lay out the letter like a business letter with the councillor's address on the top left and a topic heading.

(d)   Zappy is in a difficult situation. He will want to make his disco event sound super cool by using the right jargon. On the other hand, he will have to use quite simple language and vocabulary so that his target readers understand him. The vocabulary he uses may not have the emotive power to a foreign student that it might have to a native speaker.

Conclusion: all of these writers need to give careful thought to (a) who their readers are; (b) what they want to achieve with their piece of writing; and (c) conventions that dictate the type of text they will use.

8.3   The first writer is an adult. She explores lots of possibilities for the story and then makes quite thoughtful choices so that the story has a logical development. The second writer is a child. She plans in a straight line: she thinks of an idea, then she thinks of another idea, then another idea. She does not go back to revise what she has planned, to get an overview or to build her ideas into a story structure. One gets the feeling with the child that the logic that links the ideas is simply additive: *and . . . and . . . and*. This is what Scardamalia and Bereiter describe as KNOW-LEDGE TELLING But with the adult the planning process takes full account of cause and effect. There is evidence of KNOWLEDGE TRANS-FORMING.

Knowledge telling

Knowledge transforming

8.4 (a) If you are a good writer, you spend a lot of time planning what to say when and how to link your ideas. You probably draft and redraft what you want to say – sometimes making major changes to the structure of your essay and sometimes just polishing words. That's the joy of working on a PC.

(b) When you are writing in an exam, you are unlikely to do as much planning. You probably write linearly, like the child in Exercise 10.3: simply putting down one point after another without building them into a coherent structure.

There are two important reasons for these differences. First, in an exam you are under time pressure, whereas good writing demands adequate time for planning and revising. Second, you cannot usually use word processors in exams. You have to write by hand, which many people today find an unnatural experience. It means that you have far less scope for trying out ideas, then revising them. In short, it gives rise to a very different type of writing.

8.5 It may be that, by storing words in phonological form, we prevent them from interfering with the written words we are putting on the page. Remember that a writer has to perform two operations in parallel. They have to hold words in their mind (possibly even rehearsing the words to make sure they are not forgotten) and at the same time they have to form letters on the page.

Digraph

8.6 English sometimes uses a DIGRAPH of two letters (TH, CH, PH) to represent a sound. So does Spanish.

One English letter or digraph may represent more than one sound: TH = /θ/ and /ð/; CH = /k/ (*chemist*) and /ʧ/ (*chin*); EA = /e/ (*head*) and /iː/ (*heat*). In Spanish, it is much more common for each letter or digraph to represent only one sound.

In English, one sound can be represented in several different ways. For example, /f/ can be written as F, PH or even -GH. English vowels provide extreme examples of this: look, for example, at the number of ways of writing /iː/. In Spanish, a sound tends to be consistently represented by one letter or digraph. There are no irregular spellings like YACHT or GAUGE. Of course, Spanish speakers are helped by the fact that their language has far fewer vowels than English, so it does not need to work out variations on the basic Latin system of A-E-I-O-U.

The Spanish system is referred to as TRANSPARENT because, by looking at the written form of a word, you can work out how it is pronounced. English is relatively OPAQUE because you cannot necessarily deduce a pronunciation from a spelling.

Transparent

Opaque

8.7 (a) They would have to learn the words as a whole as there are no other words like them, in terms of the match between spelling and pronunciation.

(b) They could learn these words by ANALOGY. Once they have learnt one word ending in -IGHT, they can recognise the pattern in the spellings of others.

Analogy

(c) They have to learn two possible pronunciations: /iː/ for one group of words ending in -EAD and /e/ for the other.

(d) These words can be read aloud using basic sound–spelling rules.

Sometimes, writers and readers are able to rely upon GRAPHEME– PHONEME CORRESPONDENCE RULES (rules that link a particular sound to a particular spelling). In English, these are more reliable for conso- nants than for vowels. Sometimes, what is involved is not a single grapheme such as P or F but a digraph such as TH- or -EA-.

Grapheme– phoneme correspondence rules

Sometimes words can be acquired by analogy to other words which have apparently irregular but consistent spellings. However, some words are unique and have to be learnt as single units.

8.8 (a) Examples: PH-, CH-, SH-, -IE-, -OA-, KN-, -MB

(b) Examples: ROUGH, TOUGH, ENOUGH, SIGN, ALIGN, BENIGN, VILLAGE, CABBAGE, DAMAGE

(c) COUGH, BOUGH, TWO, WOMEN, PEOPLE

8.9 (a) These are errors of execution, where the fingers type the letters in the wrong order or put in a space too soon. They may be the result of highly automatic sequences that have been learnt wrongly.

(b) Here a word is substituted that is pronounced the same or nearly the same as the target. This confirms the idea that we hold words in our head in a phonological form.

(c) These are all function words. Writers make many mistakes when typing function words, suggesting that they pay less attention to these words (perhaps because they are so frequent) than they do to content words.

(d) These are misspellings where a writer (possibly dyslexic) does not know how to spell the words correctly and spells them as they are said.

8.10 *during their first years as writers* → *quite slowly*. Planning. The writer has changed his mind about the angle to be adopted. He decides to emphasise the slowness of the process rather than the fact that it happens early.

thye → *they* (several examples). Execution. A habitual error by this writer, who has developed a highly automatic but incorrect key sequence.

a lot of → *considerable*. Register. Change to a more formal style.

teh → *the*. Execution.

or to mouth them. Planning. The writer needed to add new information.

suggesting → *This suggests*. Stylistic. A syntactic change that helps readability by avoiding a long sentence.

mental effort is going into → *working memory is taken up with*. Register. The writer has reassessed the background knowledge of his readers, and has decided that they will recognise a term like *working memory*.

of their working memory (deleted). Stylistic. Avoiding repetition of the same words.

think ahead → *organise their ideas*. Planning. The writer has changed his ideas about the point to be made.

However. Organisational. A link is added to make the logic of the text clear.

month → *mouth*. Execution. Writer has substituted a similar key sequence.

repeat → *rehearse*. Register. Writer has decided to use a more technical term.

loose → *lose*. Execution. Phonological error.

9 THE SPEAKING PROCESS

9.1 (a) By choosing the verb PUT, the policewoman commits herself to certain sentence patterns. The most likely is PUT + object + *in/on/under* + receptacle. She knows these sentence patterns because they are stored as part of her knowledge of the word PUT.

(b)   Her knowledge of English word order.

(c)   She locates the words in her mental lexicon. She uses their meanings as her point of departure, but she may also be helped by a sense of what they are like in form (e.g. first syllable, number of syllables). See Unit 7.

(d)   She wants to express something that is happening now. So she uses this PRESENT PROGRESSIVE form of the verb. So, having chosen the verb, she has to decide how to INFLECT it.

Present progressive

Inflect

(e)   The words *he* and *the* are DEFINITE. They are used for knowledge that the speaker shares with the listener (sometimes called GIVEN knowledge). In this case, both speaker and listener have already seen the thief and the money on the video, so the speaker can refer to them as known. But the bag has obviously just appeared, so it is referred to INDEFINITELY by means of *a* rather than *the*. It is treated as new to the conversation.

Definite

Given

Indefinitely

9.2   (a)   The speaker CONTRACTS *he is* into *he's*; this is the form that we usually adopt when we are speaking.

Contracts

(b)   The speaker decides to put special stress on MONey and BAG as they are the important words of the sentence. This is known as SENTENCE STRESS.

Sentence stress

(c)   *the* and *a* have weak forms using schwa (the sound /ə/), which are much more common in speech than their full forms.

9.3   You probably found that you introduced a /j/ sound (like the first sound in *yes*) between *money* and *into* so as to make the transition between the two words easier. For similar reasons, you probably introduced a /w/ sound between *into* and *a*.

9.4   (a), (g)   When a group of consonants is difficult to say, one is sometimes omitted. This is known as ELISION.

Elision

(b), (h)   When it is difficult to move your mouth from one consonant to another, you sometimes change the first consonant to make it easier: /m/ to /p/ is easier than /n/ to /p/. This is known as ASSIMILATION.

Assimilation

(c), (e)   When a syllable begins with a vowel, the last consonant from the previous syllable is sometimes attached to it. This is known as RESYLLABIFICATION.

Resyllabification

(d), (f)   When a sequence of words occurs very often, it sometimes gets very reduced to make it easy to say as a chunk.

9.5   The jaw, the tongue, the lips. The soft palate at the back of the mouth which can be lowered to let air out through the nose (making a nasal sound). The vocal cords which are set in vibration for vowels and certain consonants. Speaking also involves the muscles that control the passage of air from the lungs.

9.6   *Conceptual stage*: she decides to comment on what is happening in the video.

Planning stage: she chooses the verb PUT, and the syntactic pattern that goes with it. She chooses the vocabulary that she needs. She uses her knowledge of word order and of inflection.

Phonological stage: she retrieves the spoken forms of the words she needs – including the weak forms of *a* and *the*.

Phonetic stage: she simplifies how she will say the words (this is optional) – maybe reducing *to* and *a* to /twə/. She forms instructions to the appropriate articulatory muscles.

Articulatory stage: she utters the words she has planned.

9.7   The speaker appears to pause quite regularly in order to plan new pieces of speech. He also makes more planning time for himself by stretching the last syllable or the last sound before he pauses. He usually

Clause   pauses after a CLAUSE – a stretch of speech that contains a verb. The clause (or sometimes the sentence) appears to be an important unit of planning in speech – though it is perhaps not the only one. It is often constructed around one or more syllables that carry heavy sentence stress.

9.8   The interviewer is more hesitant. There are four types of hesitation. The interviewer uses pauses (+) and filled pauses (*erm*). The scientist uses repetition (*it's it's*) and extends a vowel (*the*::). The interviewer makes many more pauses and the pauses very often occur in the middle of clauses rather than just at the end. So they mark hesitation rather than planning. The hesitation might arise because:

- the speaker has not planned carefully enough;
- the speaker has lost track of the plan in his buffer;
- there is a difficult word that the speaker has not managed to retrieve;
- the speaker is anxious and so tries to plan more carefully than usual or keeps checking his plan.

9.9   (a)   A grammatical error. The speaker wanted to form a question and formed a statement instead (perhaps by analogy with a sequence like *I don't know why it is that . . .*).

False start   (b)   The speaker has not planned very clearly and decides he wants to change his plan. This is known as a FALSE START.

(c)   The speaker has not made the meaning clear enough to the listeners (*you* could refer to one person or to two).

(d)   Lexical error. The speaker retrieves the wrong word.

(e)   Pronunciation error. The speaker puts the word stress on the wrong syllable.

(f)   Lexical errors. The speaker retrieves two words at the same time (*slightest* and *least*) and ends up combining them.

Most corrections occur immediately after the error, or very soon after it. Most of the examples here, such as (a), involve a correction of something that has actually been said. But (b) involves a correction of something that the speaker has planned. So it seems that we monitor what we have just said but that we also monitor our plan before we speak.

UNIT 10   LANGUAGE PROCESSING

10.1 1 b;   2 e;   3 c;   4 a;   5 d.

10.2 No. The man then has to assume that what the woman says is somehow relevant to the present situation. He has to connect her words about her own habits to the fact that he is offering her a cigarette. He interprets the underlying meaning of her utterance as being: *I'm refusing the cigarette.*

10.3 *Syllable level.* You divide the string into syllables.

[saːfpaːsnaɪn] → [saːf + paːs + naɪn]

Word form. In matching the syllables to words, you would notice that the speaker has omitted a few sounds in order to make the sequence easier to see (an example of elision: see Unit 9).

[saːf + paːs + naɪn] → [ɪts + haːf + paːst + naɪn] → IT'S HALF PAST NINE

Word meaning. HALF = ½   PAST = after   NINE = 9

Syntactic level. IT + IS (Present tense) + HALF PAST NINE
Syntactic pattern for telling the time.

Utterance meaning level.

Interpretation level. You're late.

10.4 The letters are exactly the same. What seems to affect the way you interpret them is your knowledge of the whole word.

10.5 (a)   The listener makes use of personal knowledge about the speaker. The speaker assumes that the listener knows about this woman (he uses *that*).

(b)   The listener has to use technical knowledge. The speaker assumes that they share a body of knowledge and both know what this term means.

(c)   The listener has to use knowledge of the environment in which the conversation happens. The speaker assumes that the listener knows that this shop exists.

(d)   The listener has to use knowledge of what has been said in the conversation so far. The speaker assumes that the listener has listened carefully and retained what has been said.

(e)   The listener has to draw on his/her world knowledge of elephants. The speaker assumes that the listener knows the difference between African and Asian elephants.

(f)   The listener draws on knowledge of the form of words that is used in this particular situation. The speaker assumes that the listener is familiar with this form of words and can recognise that he/she is being charged with a crime.

(g)   The listener draws on knowledge of the procedure that people go though in this kind of communicative situation. The speaker assumes that everyone present recognises the procedure.

Features

10.6 Likely replies: REVENGE/REVENUE, LONELY/LOVELY. You might have been influenced by the FEATURES of the letters (curves, horizontal lines, vertical lines, oblique lines). C has features like those of G, O like those of U. M has features like those of N, Y like those of V.

10.7 (a)   STRANGE, COMFORT, ARRIVE

(b)   GARDEN, DOMESTIC, BURGLARY

(c)   DIFFICULT, RECOVERY, HOLIDAY

(d)   THEORY, CHEERFUL, SHOCKING, PUNISH

You possibly found (a) easier because the substituted letters have features in common with the correct ones. With (c) there were no such resemblances. (b) is more difficult because it disrupts letter order. But (d) was almost certainly the most difficult. Although only one letter is replaced, the substitutions break up digraphs: TH, CH, CK, SH. Our difficulty in recognising words like those in (d) suggests that we process digraphs as a single unit.

10.8 (a)   The listener uses top-down evidence to predict what is coming next. As a result, she pays only reduced attention to the word(s) that are said.

(b)   The listener uses top-down information to work out the meaning of an ambiguous sentence, after the sentence has been heard.

(c)   The listener forms a cohort using bottom-up evidence. She then uses top-down evidence to predict the right word in the cohort.

(d)   The listener is so influenced by top-down knowledge (previous mention of carrots and potatoes, knowledge of the word VEGETABLE) that he does not notice the speaker's slip.

UNIT 11   THE READING PROCESS

11.1 Free discussion

11.2 Although English spelling is quite opaque, you can often work out how to pronounce words you have never seen before. You use the standard relationships between letters and sounds (known as grapheme–phoneme correspondence rules).

11.3 GEAD (a) /giːd/ (perhaps /dʒiːd/) (cf.: BEAD, READ) or (b) /ged/ (perhaps /dʒed/) (cf.: HEAD, DEAD);

NEAN /niːn/;

SOAT /səʊt/;

PIVE (a) /pɪv/ (b) /paɪv/;

FOWN (a) /faʊn/ or (b) /fəʊn/;

HEAF (a) /hiːf/ or (b) /hef/;

WIRT /wɜːt/.

You probably arrived at these pronunciations by analogy: by comparing the non-words with actual words that you know in English. This is another important method for working out the pronunciation of an unknown word. Readers seem to be especially aware of the RIME part of **Rime** single-syllable words (the vowel and the last consonant or consonants).

11.4 NEAN /niːn/ MEAN, DEAN, BEAN, LEAN, WEAN, CLEAN

SOAT /səʊt/ GOAT, MOAT, BOAT, FLOAT, THROAT

PIVE /pɪv/ GIVE, LIVE (vb); /paɪv/ DIVE, FIVE, LIVE (adj.), DRIVE

FOWN /faʊn/ GOWN, DOWN, FROWN, TOWN, DROWN, CROWN; /fəʊn/ MOWN, GROWN, KNOWN, SOWN, BLOWN, SHOWN

HEAF /hiːf/ LEAF, SHEAF; /hef/ DEAF

WIRT /wɜːt/ DIRT, SHIRT, SKIRT

You are more likely to choose a pronunciation that represents a large set of neighbours or a set of very frequent neighbours.

11.5 It seems that neither 'whole word' nor 'phonics' is enough on its own. The child who is learning to read needs three different types of approach:

- 'whole word' for rapid reading and so that words like YACHT can be recognised;
- 'phonics' so that a sub-lexical route can be established both for letters and for digraphs like -EA- or TH- – enabling new words to be pronounced;
- analogy, so that words with similar spellings can be linked in the lexicon.

11.6 (a)   The figure usually quoted for English is 7 to 9.

(b)   None.

(c)   Function words. Either because they are very frequent and thus easily recognised or because they are very short.

(d)   By taking in a very general impression of the letters and space that lie ahead, the reader can work out where to put the next fixation point (how long is the next word?) and whether to skip a short function word.

(e)   Long words (*creativity*), infrequent words, and words which are a little odd in their context (*drivers, payoff, good news*).

(f)   The first time (*healthy body may*), the reader has made too big a saccade. The second time, the reader has made quite a big saccade, and then has to check on a rather complex syntactic pattern (*for all those who*). The third time, the reader seems to be checking on a complex word: *activity*.

11.7, 11.8   You probably found that you read Text B faster than Text A. In Text A the vocabulary is less frequent, and the links between the ideas are more complex. Your fixations may at times have been quite long (checking words, checking understanding) and you may have regressed occasionally. With Text B, your fixations were probably shorter and there was less regression.

Text A is a different *type* of text from Text B, demanding a different type of reading. Text B may have seemed shorter than Text A. In fact, Text A has 140 words while Text B has 172.

11.9 1 (c);   2 (d);   3 (b);   4 (a).

11.10 See the features mentioned after the exercise as characteristic of a weak reader.

11.11 Weak readers regress because they need to check whether they have decoded words accurately. Good readers regress to check that they have understood correctly.

11.12 See the commentary after the exercise. The task you have just done is an adaptation of a famous psychological technique, the Stroop test. In its original form, words such as RED or BLUE are written in various coloured inks, and the subject has to report not what the word is but what colour ink it is written in.

11.13 You will find that relatively few words can be predicted. The figures often quoted suggest that no more than about 40 per cent of function words and 10 per cent of content words can be predicted from context. How does this compare with your results?

11.14 Anticipating is much more costly. If we used anticipating instead of decoding, it would leave much less working memory for building overall meaning and for interpreting the text.

PROJECT: When you have your results, you may like to compare them with those that Philip Gough and Sebastian Wren obtained. See pages 59–64 of their article 'Constructing meaning: the role of decoding'. You will find it in J. Oakhill and R. Beard (eds): *Reading Development and the Teaching of Reading*. Oxford: Blackwell, 1999.

UNIT 12   THE LISTENING PROCESS

12.1 *Margaret*   How many cigars do you smoke in a day?
  Henry   [I] can't say exactly. About two or three, perhaps. Perhaps three.
  Margaret   Henry, one does wish you'd try to smoke less. Such big cigars, too. [I'm] sure it can't be good for one. Surely one can remember what Charles said about your heart.
  Henry   Yes, dear. Yes dear, of course.
  Margaret   Henry, promise me you'll try to cut them down to two a day.

12.2 Accent. The way many words are reduced. Weak forms for function words which make them quite difficult to recognise. Difficulty in working out where words begin and end. Omission of words.

12.3 (a) The distinctive features of the letters (lines, curves etc.); gaps between the letters.

(b) Gaps between the words.

(c) Commas (sometimes); often nothing.

(d) Commas (often).

(e) Full stops.

(f) Bold or italic typeface.

12.4 No gaps between words. No punctuation to help mark clause/ sentence boundaries. Important words are stressed. Sounds can be missed out. Some sounds are reduced to weak /ə/.

12.5 (a) A syllable has certain standard forms. They can be as simple as (V = vowel, C = consonant):

V (*I*); CV (*me*); VC (*us*).

Closed But most syllables in English are CLOSED, with at least one consonant at the beginning and at least one at the end:

CVC (*him*), CCVC (*stop*), CCCVC (*strip*) etc.

(b) There are no regular gaps between words.

Intonation (c) INTONATION helps to mark the ends of some phrases and many clauses and sentences. Planning pauses often mark the ends of clauses and sentences.

Sentence stress (d) SENTENCE STRESS marks which words are important in the message.

12.6 With NEXT and PLATFORM, the speaker has made it easier to say the words by missing out one of the sounds. With SEVEN, the speaker has made it easier to say the word by substituting a /b/ for the /v/. The function words FOR, THE and FROM are said in their weak forms: /fə/ /ðə/ /frəm/. This is how they are normally said in everyday speech.

These simplifications would seem to make life easier for the speaker but harder for the listener.

12.7 (a) The consonants are roughly where the dark bars are uneven and the vowels are where the bars remain relatively horizontal. So

Steady-state vowels can often be distinguished because they are STEADY-STATE: the features remain constant.

(b) No. They blend into each other.

(c) No. It varies according to the vowel that follows it.

(d) You use the back of your tongue (and the back part of your mouth) for the /k/ in CAT. You use the front for the /k/ in KIT. So there are really two sounds, but we hear them both as /k/.

12.8 Maybe we have a 'good' version of /k/ in our minds. Wherever we hear a variation, we match it against the prototype to see how closely it resembles it.

12.9 /kən/ in **con**sumption, re**ckon**

/ɪks/ in ex**ci**ting, phys**ics**

/sʌm/ in con**sum**ption, **som**ebody

/ʃən/ in consump**tion**, Egyp**tian**

/tɪŋ/ in exci**ting**, **tin**ker

This suggests that languages have syllables which recur quite frequently in different words.

12.10 (a) Women's voices are usually higher in pitch than men's.

(b) Children's voices are usually higher in pitch than those of adults.

(c) There are different regional accents.

(d) People speak more carefully in a formal situation. They often speak more slowly and may even change their accent.

(e) People are likely to speak faster when they are excited and faster and louder when they are angry. They are likely to speak less coherently, with more pausing, when they are tired or worried.

(a) to (c) reflect the speaker; (d) and (e) reflect the situation.

12.11 pitch: (a), (b) and (e); speed: (d) and (e); loudness: (d) and (e); pausing: (d) and (e); phonemes: (c); intonation: (c), (d) and (e).

12.12 thecaptain'sincabin: the + cap + tin + zinc + abin?

incabinsixteen: in + cab + in + six + teen

12.13 (a) the waiter cut it/the way to cut it

(b) went to a sister/went to assist her

(c) attacks on the people/a tax on the people

(d) we can fast/weaken fast/weak and fast

12.14 thə + **necks** + trainfə + **LON**dən + isthəsebm + **FOR**tyfrəm + pla'form + **EIGHT**

(a) the + WAIter + CUTit

(b) +WENTtoa + SISter

(c) a + TAXonthe + PEOPle

(d) WEAKen + FAST

12.15 PHOtograph – photoGRAPHic – phoTOGraphy

Speakers of Hungarian and Czech can segment connected speech *before* each stressed syllable.

Speakers of Persian can segment connected speech *after* each stressed syllable.

Speakers of Bahasa Indonesia know that a content word will end on the syllable after the stressed one.

GLOSSARY OF LINGUISTIC TERMS

adjective a word that describes a person, animal, object or abstract concept.

agree describes the way in which one constituent of a sentence changes to conform with another constituent. Example, in the sentence *My sister likes chocolate*, the word *like* has *-s* added to make it agree with *my sister* (singular). Think also of the way adjectives have to agree with nouns in French.

antonym a word with the opposite sense to another.

auxiliary a verb that adds grammatical information to the main verb. Examples: She *is* listening; I *have* finished.

clause a unit of grammatical structure containing a verb.

collocate a word that often occurs with another.

collocation the frequent co-occurrence of two words.

common noun any noun apart from those which are names of people, cities, countries etc.

consonant a sound made by narrowing or closing the vocal tract.

content word a word that has dictionary meaning (as against a word that has mainly a grammatical function).

contracted shortened form of a verb. Examples: *I have* → *I've*
I am → *I'm*.

converse a word that reverses a relationship represented by another word. Example: BUY is the converse of SELL. A buys a car from B; B sells the car to A.

countable noun a noun representing an object that can be counted – i.e. that potentially has a plural.

definiteness a way of marking something as known. The best example is *the*, the definite article, which a speaker uses when talking about something that has already been introduced into the conversation or that is regarded as known to the listener.

derivational marking the way in which one word is derived from another. It describes the role of (e.g.) UN- in UNHAPPY or -NESS in HAPPINESS. Contrasted with **inflectional**.

digraph a unit of two letters representing a single sound. Examples: TH-, -EA-.

discourse a continuous stretch of language larger than a sentence.

false start occurs when a speaker begins a sentence in a certain way, then changes his/her plan and has to start the sentence again.

filler meaningless expressions such as *well, you know*, which give a speaker time to plan.

formal a situation that demands some care in constructing sentences and selecting appropriate vocabulary.

formulaic chunks sequences like *How do you do?* where the words do not have individual meaning and the sequence is produced as if it were a single unit.

frequency how common a word is.

frequency how high or low a voice is, as measured by an instrument.

function word a word that serves a grammatical function and has little or no meaning. Examples: *the, of, it*.

'given' already mentioned or established in an earlier part of a conversation or written text.

grammar a set of rules that determine the syntax of a language (how words are combined) and its morphology (how words are marked to show their grammatical functions. Example: WALK – WALKED).

grammatical word see **function word**.

grapheme a unit of writing: in an alphabetic system, a letter.

hyponym a word that belongs to the category referred to by another word. Example: SPARROW is a hyponym of BIRD.

impersonal structure a sentence pattern based on *It + is/was + adjective + that*. Example: *It's strange that she's so late*.

indefinite treated as not previously mentioned and not known to the reader/listener. Compare: *a book* (indefinite) and *the/that book* (definite).

inflection a prefix or suffix added to a word form to mark its grammatical function. Example: plural *-s* in BOOKS, past tense *-ed* in WALKED.

intensity how loud a voice is, as measured by an instrument.

intonation the pattern made by the changing pitch (high–low) of a speaker's voice. The focus of an intonation contour is a syllable that carries sentence stress in the form of a very marked pitch movement.

lexical stress an emphasis that falls on one syllable of any English word of two or more syllables. Examples: *LITerature, geOGraphy, matheMATics*.

lexis vocabulary.

loudness   how loud a voice is, as heard by a listener.

meronym   a word that represents a part of what is represented by another word. ELBOW is a meronym of ARM.

morphology   the study of the structure of words. Includes the use of prefixes and suffixes to add information to words. Distinguish inflectional morphology (supplying information about grammatical roles) from derivational morphology (creating new words from existing ones).

negative   opposite of a positive statement. Examples: I *didn't* enjoy it. I *don't* know him.

negative question   Example: *Didn't you enjoy it?*

'new'   a topic that is introduced into a conversation or a text for the first time.

noun   a word that refers to an object, person, animal, substance or abstract idea. Capable of being the subject of a sentence.

object   the noun or noun phrase that is controlled by the verb of the sentence. Example: *Mary* in *John phoned Mary.*

phoneme   a sound of a language which serves to distinguish minimally different words: thus, the phoneme /p/ distinguishes PIN from BIN, TIN and SIN.

phonetics   the study of the actual sounds that speakers produce (as compared with the system that underlies the sounds).

phonology   the sound system of a language, represented by contrasts between phonemes.

phrase   a group of words which hang together syntactically. Examples: *the woman in the car, just in time, afraid of ghosts.* Traditionally, a distinction is made between a clause, which has a verb in it, and a phrase, which does not.

pitch   how high or low a voice is, as perceived by a listener.

plural   in English, more than one (BOOKS as against BOOK).

prefix   a unit smaller than a word which can be added to the beginning of a word to modify it or to provide additional information. Example: UN- in UNHAPPY.

preposition   a word that links a noun or noun phrase to the remainder of a sentence. Examples: *in* (the woman *in* the car – he is sitting *in* the restaurant), *of* (a bottle *of* milk – I'm afraid *of* dogs).

present progressive   a form of the verb in English that tells us about an event or activity that is in progress now. Example: *I'm reading a book.*

progressive   a verb form used in English to show that an action is or was in progress. Example: *I am driving a car* as compared with *I drive a car.*

proper noun   a noun that is the name of a person, town, country etc. Usually marked in English by an initial capital letter.

proposition   a unit of meaning, a single abstract idea.

root   the central part of a word which remains when prefixes and suffixes have been taken off. Example: -WEAK- in UNWEAKENED.

sentence stress   stress that highlights the most important word in a group of words linked by a single intonation pattern. It is usually shown by a marked change in the pitch (high–low) of the speaker's voice. Examples: *Who are you meeting on Saturday? – I'm meeting JOHN on Saturday./When are you meeting John? – I'm meeting John on SATurday*. Distinguish from lexical stress on individual words.

subject   the noun or noun phrase that controls the verb of a sentence. Example: *John* in *John phoned Mary*.

suffix   a unit, smaller than a word, that can be added to the end of a word to modify it or to provide additional information. Example: -NESS in HAPPINESS.

superordinate   a word that describes the category of which another word is a member. INSECT is the superordinate of CATERPILLAR.

syllable   a unit of speech or writing with a vowel sound at its centre. It can have one or more consonants at the beginning or the end.

synonym   a word that has the same sense as another.

syntactic structure   the grammatical pattern of a phrase, clause or sentence.

syntax   the way in which the rules of grammar combine words into phrases, clauses and sentences.

tag question   a request for confirmation added on to a statement. Example: You know him, *don't you?*

turn   a continuous stretch of speech by one speaker in a conversation.

verb   a word that refers to an action, activity or state.

verb form   a variant of the standard form (stem) of a verb. In English, the form might reflect the time of an event (WALK – WALKED) or a concept like progressivity (WALK – I AM WALKING).

vowel   a sound that is made without blocking the air in the mouth or narrowing the air so as to create friction.

word order   the order in which the different parts of a sentence are usually arranged when forming a statement (rather than a question). In English, the order is usually SVO (subject-verb-object). In other languages, it may be SOV or VSO.

word-class   the category to which a word belongs, as determined by its grammatical function. Examples: noun, verb, preposition, adjective.

FURTHER READING

CHAPTER 1

Aitchison, J. *The Articulate Mammal*. London: Routledge, 1998. 4th edn. Chap. 2.
Dobrovolsky, M. 'Animal communication'. In W. O'Grady, M. Dobrovolsky and F. Katamba (eds) *Contemporary Linguistics*. Harlow: Longman, 1996. 3rd edn.
Savage-Rumbaugh, E.S. and Lewin, R. *Kanzi: At the Brink of the Human Mind*. New York: Wiley, 1994.

CHAPTER 2

Aitchison, J. *The Articulate Mammal*. London: Routledge, 1998. 4th edn. Chap. 3; pp. 85–90.
Cattell, R. *Children's Language: Consensus and Controversy*. London: Cassell, 2000. Chaps 9–10.
Hale, S. *The Man who Lost his Language*. London: Penguin, 2003.
Libben, G. 'Brain and language'. In W. O'Grady, M. Dobrovolsky and F. Katamba (eds) *Contemporary Linguistics*. Harlow: Longman, 1996. 3rd edn.
Obler, L.K. and Gjerlow, K. *Language and the Brain*. Cambridge: Cambridge University Press, 1999.
Ratey, J. *A User's Guide to the Human Brain*. London: Abacus, 2003.

CHAPTER 3

Aitchison, J. *The Articulate Mammal*. London: Routledge, 1998. 4th edn. Chaps 4–6.

Cattell, R. *Children's Language: Consensus and Controversy*. London: Cassell, 2000. Chaps 3, 5 and 6.

Foster-Cohen, S.H. *An Introduction to Child Language Development*. Harlow: Longman, 1999. Chaps 1, 5 and 7.

CHAPTER 4

Aitchison, J. *The Articulate Mammal*. London: Routledge, 1998. 4th edn. Chap. 7.

Cattell, R. *Children's Language: Consensus and Controversy*. London: Cassell, 2000. Chaps 7, 13–15.

Foster, S.H. *The Communicative Competence of Young Children*. Harlow: Longman, 1990. Chap. 4.

Foster-Cohen, S.H. *An Introduction to Child Language Development*. Harlow: Longman, 1999. Chaps 4 and 6.

Peccei, J. *Child Language*. London: Routledge Language Workbooks, 1994.

CHAPTER 5

Cattell, R. *Children's Language: Consensus and Controversy*. London: Cassell, 2000. Chap. 15.

Ellis, A.W. *Reading, Writing and Dyslexia*. Hove: Psychology Press, 1993. 2nd edn.

Foster-Cohen, S.H. *An Introduction to Child Language Development*. Harlow: Longman, 1999. Chap. 6.

Newton, M. *Savage Girls and Wild Boys*. London: Faber & Faber, 2002.

CHAPTER 6

Aitchison, J. *Words in the Mind*. Oxford: Blackwell, 1998. 2nd edn. Chaps 1–6, 8, 9 and 11.

Coates, R. *Word Structure*. London: Routledge Language Workbooks, 1999.

McCarthy, M. *Vocabulary*. Oxford: Oxford University Press, 1990. Chaps 1 and 2.

CHAPTER 7

Aitchison, J. *Words in the Mind*. Oxford: Blackwell, 2003. 3rd edn. Chaps 12, 18–20.

Gradoll, D., Cheshire, J. and Swann, J. *Describing Language*. Milton Keynes: Open University, 1994. 2nd edn, pp. 102–115.

McCarthy, M. *Vocabulary*. Oxford: Oxford University Press, 1990. Chap. 3.

CHAPTER 8

Halliday, M.A.K. *Spoken and Written Language*. Oxford: Oxford University Press, 1989. 2nd edn.

Scardamalia, M. and Bereiter, B. 'Knowledge telling and knowledge transforming in written composition'. In S. Rosenberg (ed.) *Advances in Applied Psycholinguistics*. Cambridge: Cambridge University Press, 1987.

Tribble, C. *Writing*. Oxford: Oxford University Press, 1996. Chaps 1–6.

CHAPTER 9

Ellis, A. and Beattie, G. *The Psychology of Language and Communication*. Hove: Erlbaum, 1986. Chaps 7 and 8, pp. 115–150.

Scovel, T. *Psycholinguistics*. Oxford: Oxford University Press, 1998. Chap. 3.

CHAPTER 10

Carroll, D. *Psychology of Language*. Pacific Grove, CA: Brooks Cole, 1999. 3rd edn, pp. 50–57.

Field, J. *Psycholinguistics: the Key Concepts*. Routledge, 2004. Entries for: 'bottom-up processing', 'top-down processing'.

CHAPTER 11

Ellis, A.W. *Reading, Writing and Dyslexia*. Hove: Psychology Press, 1993.

Goswami, U. and Bryant, P. *Phonological Skills and Learning to Read*. Oxford: Oxford University Press, 1990.

Oakhill, J. and Garnham, A. *Becoming a Skilled Reader*. Oxford: Blackwell, 1988.

Oakhill, J. and Beard, R. (eds) *Reading Development and the Teaching of Reading*. Oxford: Blackwell, 1999.

CHAPTER 12

Ellis, A. and Beattie, G. *The Psychology of Language and Communication.* Hove: Erlbaum, 1986. Chap. 12.

Field, J. *Psycholinguistics.* London: Routledge English Language Introductions, 2003. pp. 30–33.

Rost, M. *Introducing Listening.* London: Penguin, 1994.

REFERENCES AND SOURCES

Aitchison, J. and Straf, M. (1982) 'Lexical storage and retrieval: a developing skill'. *Linguistics*, 19: 751–795.

Boomer, D.S. and Laver, J.D.M. (1968) 'Slips of the tongue'. Reprinted in V.A. Fromkin (ed.) *Errors in Linguistic Performance: Slips of the Tongue, Ear, Pen and Hand*. New York: Academic Press.

Brown, R. (1973) *A First Language: The Early Stages*. London: George Allen & Unwin.

Chomsky, N. (1959) 'Review of B.F. Skinner's *Verbal Behavior*'. *Language*, 35: 16–58.

Chomsky, N. (1965) *Aspects of the Theory of Syntax*. Cambridge, MA: MIT Press.

Christie, A. (1936) *The ABC Murders*. London: Collins.

Curtiss, S. (1977) *Genie: A Psycholinguistic Study of a Modern-day 'Wild Child'*. New York: Academic Press.

Cutler, A. (1980) 'Errors of stress and intonation'. In V.A. Fromkin (ed.) *Errors in Linguistic Performance: Slips of the Tongue, Ear, Pen and Hand*. New York: Academic Press.

Deacon, T. (1997) *The Symbolic Species*. London: Penguin.

Ellis, A.W. (1993) *Reading, Writing and Dyslexia*. Hove: Psychology Press, 2nd edn.

Ferguson, C. (1977) 'Baby talk as a simplified register'. In C.E. Snow and C.A. Ferguson (eds) *Talking to Children*. Cambridge: Cambridge University Press.

Fletcher, P. (1988) *A Child's Learning of English*. Oxford: Blackwell.

Foster-Cohen, S.H. (1999) *An Introduction to Child Language Development*. London: Longman.

Fromkin, V.A. (1973) *Speech Errors as Linguistic Evidence*. The Hague: Mouton.

Funnell, E. (1983) 'Ideographic communication and word-class differences in aphasia'. Unpublished PhD thesis, University of Reading.

Goodman, K. (1967) 'Reading: a psycholinguistic guessing game'. *Journal of the Reading Specialist*, 6: 126–135.

Kimura, D. (1961) 'Cerebral dominance and the perception of verbal stimuli'. *Canadian Journal of Psychology*, 15: 166–171.

Langford, D. (1994) *Analysing Talk*. Basingstoke: Macmillan.

Lauder, A. (1968) *Fraffly Well Spoken*. London: Wolfe Publishing.

Leech, G., Rayson, P. and Wilson, A. (2001) *Word Frequencies in Written and Spoken English*. Harlow: Pearson.

Levelt, W. (1989) *Speaking*. Cambridge, MA: MIT Press.

MacWhinney, B. (2000) *The CHILDES Project: Tools for Analyzing Talk*. Mahwah, NJ: Lawrence Erlbaum Associates.

Miles, T.R. (1993) *Dyslexia: The Pattern of Difficulties*. London: Whurr, 2nd edn.

Newport, E., Gleitman, H. and Gleitman, L. (1977) 'Mother, I'd rather do it myself: some effects and noneffects of maternal speech style'. In C. Snow and C. Ferguson (eds) *Talking to Children: Language Input and Acquisition*. Cambridge: Cambridge University Press.

Peters, A.M. (1983) *The Units of Language Acquisition*. New York: Cambridge University Press.

Rasmussen, T. and Milner, B. (1977) 'Clinical and surgical studies of the cerebral speech areas in man'. In K.J. Zulch, O. Creutzfeldt and G.C. Galbraith (eds) *Cerebral Localization*. New York: Springer Verlag, pp. 238–257.

Rayner, K. and Pollatsek, A. (1989) *The Psychology of Reading*. Englewood Cliffs, NJ: Prentice Hall.

Rosch, E. (1975) 'Cognitive representations of semantic categories'. *Journal of Experimental Psychology: General*, 104: 192–233.

Savage-Rumbaugh, E.S. and Lewin, R. (1994) *Kanzi: At the Brink of the Human Mind*. New York: Wiley.

Rumelhardt, D.E. and McClelland, J.L. (1986) *Parallel Distributed Processing*, Vol 1. Cambridge, MA: MIT Press.

Scardamalia, M. and Bereiter, C. (1987) 'Knowledge telling and knowledge transforming in written composition'. In S. Rosenberg (ed.) *Advances in Applied Psycholinguistics, Vol. 2*. Cambridge: Cambridge University Press.

Skinner, B.F. (1957) *Verbal Behavior*. Englewood Cliffs, NJ: Prentice Hall.

Snow, C. (1986) 'Conversations with children'. In P. Fletcher and M. Garman (eds) *Language Acquisition*. New York: Cambridge University Press, 2nd edn.

Underwood, M. (1975) *Listen to This!* Oxford: Oxford University Press, 2nd edn.

INDEX OF PSYCHOLINGUISTIC TERMS

References are to Unit numbers

eBooks – at www.eBookstore.tandf.co.uk

A library at your fingertips!

eBooks are electronic versions of printed books. You can store them on your PC/laptop or browse them online.

They have advantages for anyone needing rapid access to a wide variety of published, copyright information.

eBooks can help your research by enabling you to bookmark chapters, annotate text and use instant searches to find specific words or phrases. Several eBook files would fit on even a small laptop or PDA.

NEW: Save money by eSubscribing: cheap, online access to any eBook for as long as you need it.

Annual subscription packages

We now offer special low-cost bulk subscriptions to packages of eBooks in certain subject areas. These are available to libraries or to individuals.

For more information please contact webmaster.ebooks@tandf.co.uk

We're continually developing the eBook concept, so keep up to date by visiting the website.

www.eBookstore.tandf.co.uk